MAN
in the City
of the Future

STUDIES OF THE MODERN CORPORATION
Columbia University, Graduate School of Business

Francis Joseph Aguilar, *Scanning the Business Environment*

Herman W. Bevis, *Corporate Financial Reporting in a Competitive Economy*

Richard Eells, *The Corporation and the Arts*

Richard Eells and **Clarence Walton,** *Man in the City of the Future*

Albert S. Glickman, Clifford P. Hahn, Edwin A. Fleishman and **Brent Baxter,** *Top Management Development and Succession: An Exploratory Study*

Jay W. Lorsch, *Product Innovation and Organization*

Kenneth G. Patrick and **Richard Eells,** *Education and the Business Dollar*

Irving Pfeffer, *The Financing of Small Business*

George A. Steiner, *Top Management Planning*

George A. Steiner and **Warren M. Cannon,** *Multinational Corporate Planning*

George A. Steiner and **William G. Ryan,** *Industrial Project Management*

Gus Tyler, *The Political Imperative: The Corporate Character of Unions*

Clarence Walton and **Richard Eells,** *The Business System* (3 volumes)

Man in the City of the Future

A Symposium of Lions International
at the University of Puerto Rico

MAN
IN THE CITY
OF THE FUTURE

A Symposium of Urban Philosophers

Richard Eells and Clarence Walton, Editors

AN ARKVILLE PRESS BOOK

THE MACMILLAN COMPANY

COLLIER-MACMILLAN LIMITED, LONDON

—————to the service of man

Studies of the Modern Corporation

Columbia University, Graduate School of Business

The Program for Studies of the Modern Corporation is devoted to the advancement and dissemination of knowledge about the corporation. Because of the historic nexus between the merchant and the metropolis, it is both logical and appropriate to include in its series of publications a collection of essays written by distinguished contemporary urban philosophers on topics related to the problems and prospects of the city.

Both the city and the corporation have their disparagers and their eulogists. What is now required is the balanced work of their expositors. Especially needed today is a thoroughgoing contextual exposition of the roles of these institutions in the great transformations of contemporary life. We need to know what the city and the corporation are doing to the cherished values in a society of free men, whether they strengthen or weaken the individual in his struggle against the destructive forces of his local, national and global environment, and how man can more effectively use these social artifacts to achieve humanity for himself and solidarity with his fellow-man.

Publications of the Program are designed to stimulate inquiry, research, criticism, and reflection. They fall into four categories: works by outstanding businessmen, scholars, and professional men from a variety of backgrounds and academic disciplines; prizewinning doctoral dissertations relating to the corporation; annotated and edited selections of business literature; and business classics that merit republication. The studies are supported by outside grants from private business, professional and philanthropic institutions interested in the Program's objectives.

Richard Eells
EDITOR

Foreword

The problems of the city have achieved a magnitude of attention equal to that raised over issues associated with the reform movement of the 1890's. The subject and the cause have been taken up by the press, and proposed solutions can no longer be local in scope because cities have become the nations' primary claimants. In recent months the nations of the world through their statesmen, their legislators, businessmen, sociologists, commentators and scholars have spoken on the critical problems usually identified as the "urban crisis."

Concern with the problems of the cities, therefore, is more than simple idealism or passing academic fancy: it stems from fear and great apprehension. The apprehension is born of the sure knowledge that if urban problems are left to chance or to indifference the results will necessarily be tragic. We see in the great cities of the world a palpable disintegration: they are places where a man can no longer live in safety, with convenience, with a sense of security or with a feeling of human dignity.

Yet the city has been absolutely fundamental to contemporary civilization. It is safe to suggest, therefore, that domestic progress through the remainder of this century will depend heavily upon ability to derive imaginative new solutions to the great problems we now face. It is most appropriate to have had such a fundamental inquiry and academic program take place here in San Juan, Puerto Rico, which is literally a city at the crossroads of the Western Hemisphere. In many ways San Juan might be viewed as a microcosm of the ills that beset other urban areas.

It is most fitting that The International Association of Lions Clubs Board of Directors considered a discussion of urban problems that are exceedingly important to the community of man. It was this conviction that led the Board to invite a panel of renowned authorities to meet at the University of San Juan to discuss problems of urban life. From this symposium the Lions will be able to marshal an army of nearly one million men of good-will to stimulate interest and to influence the thinking of community leaders around the world of issues related to the future of the city.

We are grateful for the participation of Professor Richard Eells and Dean Clarence Walton of Columbia University who served as Symposium Coordinator and Program Moderator, respectively.

We are grateful for an opportunity once more to be of service to mankind.

Jorge Bird
President of The International
Association of Lions Clubs 1967-68

CONTENTS

XIII

1

Richard Eells and Clarence Walton

Introduction:
The Exciting
and Explosive City

A short three decades hence man will cross the most exciting of Time's many thresholds: a new millennium. For modern man, as well as for the ancient Greeks, the very idea of the *chiloi* (the Greek word for "thousand"), exerts an irresistible and nerve-tingling allure. Even in religion, and despite the fact that no Christian church formally approved the idea, the millennium has been anticipated by those who believe in the second coming of Christ who would be the King of peace during the next 1,000 years. This Christian vision is not too dissimilar from Plato's Myth of Er in the *Republic* which foretold the return of departed souls after their purification during a thousand-year existence in another world.

Whether the year 2000 will represent substantial fulfillment of utopian dreams or descent to catastrophe will be determined by what man does over the next three decades. Because contemporary man, Janus-like, glances simultaneously both forward and backward at his multitudinous problems, his prophecies are always molded by his experiences. In considering, for example, the problem of population

1

growth, he looks backward to gain the perspective necessary to realize how truly dramatic this growth has been. It took thousands of years for mankind to increase his kind by over a billion. Yet this phenomenon was achieved within the score of years running from 1945 to 1965, when the population jumped from 2.3 to 3.3 billion. Indeed, if we take modestly into account only the 3 per cent population increase rate of the developing countries, it is clear that another billion human beings will be on the face of the earth by 1980. (See the accompanying graph.) Never before in the history of mankind has the world added one billion people in a fifteen-year span!

Twenty Centuries of World Population Growth

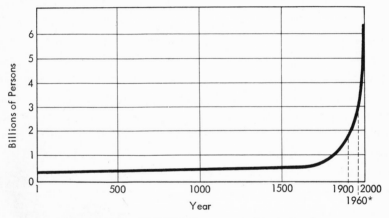

*Projected from 1960 [U.S. Department of Agriculture]

A growth rate of 3 per cent annually means that the population would double within a generation and multiply eighteen-fold within a century. If the mind recoils at statistics of such magnitude, the lesson is driven realistically home by a more manageable comparison: each year the world's population increases by over fifty million and, in the process, creates a country equivalent to England, France, or Italy. Within this framework, too, the United States creates monthly a city the size of Toledo and each year adds a new Philadelphia. In one of the following essays James W. Rouse makes this point: "Since 1940 Baltimore added to its population a city larger than Milwaukee. In the next twenty years it will add another city about the size of Miami. And in the same period of time Washington, thirty-five miles away, will be adding a city as large as Baltimore."

Recognition of the further fact that four-fifths of the future population growth will occur in underdeveloped areas of the world makes it imperative to take a hard look at patterns in Latin America, Africa, and Asia. In these underdeveloped areas, the number of inhabitants of cities of 500,000 or over more than tripled between 1940 and 1960, and it is expected that by 2000 nearly 47 per cent of the population of Latin America may be living in cities of this size. If the experiences of the 'fifties are any guide—when Mexico City, São Paulo, Bogotá, Guayaquil, and Quito more than doubled their populations—then the projections for urban growth in the future must be taken seriously by policy planners in both the public and private sectors.

The dream of building a greater and nobler city is an essential element of all utopian schemes. In one of the more persuasive assessments of urban history, Lewis Mumford noted the fact that all utopias, from Plato to Bellamy, have been expressed largely in terms of the city. As a student of both utopias and cities, Mumford came to the conclusion that the very concept of a utopia is not a Hellenic speculative fancy, but rather a derivation from a historic event, so that "the first Utopia was a city itself."[1] The formation of the city is a social innovation whose long history demonstrates a fascinating interplay between the spiritual-cultural forces of the society and its economic component. A sketch of the evolution of that relationship provides interesting perspectives.

BUSINESS AND THE PREINDUSTRIAL CITY

It was about 3000 B.C. that the first cities that had a directly traceable impact on contemporary Western culture came into being. These early cities were the result of a gathering-together of villages under the leadership of a nomadic hunter who then became the stationary

3

protective leader for the security-seeking peasant. Because the hunter-king periodically waged war against other rural villages and other cities, the need for a protective wall soon became apparent. In addition to providing defense, however, the wall permitted the performance of three crucial functions within the city: enclosure, assembly, and creativity.[2] Security from outside attack meant a release from the drudgery of guard duty and soldiering, and the consequent release of free time enabled a city dweller to use his leisure in creatively productive fashions.

The city thus became the center for art, thought, and other enriching personal relationships; it was a promise of something "more than a purely functional organization for factories and warehouses, barracks, courts, prisons, and control centers. The towers and domes of the historic city are reminders of that still unfulfilled promise."[3] These ancient cities eventually were replaced by the Greek city-states that flourished between the seventh and fourth centuries B.C. In every city was an acropolis, and this home of the city's gods served as the center of most activities. Eventually, and consistently, the acropolis was superseded as the civic center by the *agora,* or market place.

Even in that early day the city was home to the two kinds of men (often remarked upon by modern writers as uniquely characteristic of our own technological age) namely, the men of thought and the men of action.[4] The Greek philosophers, concerned with freedom and growth of the intellect, were the men of thought who remained skeptical of traders; as a consequence only foreigners were allowed to hold such "low" assignments. But these foreign businessmen, these men of action, were much like their nineteenth-century followers in that they were somewhat indifferent to the type of government so long as they could carry out their business and earn a profit. But the important item to note is that consistently the *agora* tended to replace the acropolis as the center for law and government, industry and sociability.

In one sense the Romans used the forum as the Greeks had employed the *agora*—namely, as centers of business and administration, justice and religion. But it was scarcely the spirit of business entre-

4

preneurship that permeated Roman value structures. By 350 A.D., prior to the downfall of the Empire, the total number of public holidays had jumped to over 200 or more per year; conspicuous consumption, deteriorating housing, high rents, dense crowds, exploitation of distant territories, and mass spectacles had become characteristic in the nation of parasites. Rome is a story of a city of a million people during the first century reduced to a city of 17,000 in the fourteenth.

Although a marriage of necessity rather than convenience, the relationship between the religiocultural forces, on one hand, and business, on the other, did not lead to a happy union under Christian influence. St. John Chrysostom (347-407) declared that "no Christian ought to be a merchant, and if he should wish to become one, he should be ejected from the house of God!"[5] And when the towns began to grow in the eleventh and twelfth centuries, they did so under the leadership of businessmen whose influence led St. Thomas Aquinas (1225-1274) to declare that "a good society ought to moderately employ merchants." These old tensions were weakened somewhat by the Renaissance and by the Enlightenment because both intensified the secularization of life. It was this cultural climate (attended by a kind of humanism that stressed the materialistic aspects of life and a kind of intellectualism that emphasizes quantification) that made the transit from an agrarian to an industrial society possible.

Yet even in the preindustrial world there developed patterns to serve as interesting prototypes. For example, London of the eighteenth century represented an area with a fairly distinct preindustrial ecology: in the town's center were concentrated status households whereas lower-status families were bunched along the periphery and outside the London Walls. What was true of London in 1720 appeared to be true of early twentieth-century America because in 1920 Lord Bryce described the American city of that age as an area with a center "appropriated by the richest sort, fifteen or twenty, and then stretching out into the suburbs which were filled with the dwellings of the poor."[6] It took a century and a half for this pattern to be reversed in England; it took less than a third of this time for the same thing to occur in the

United States. Today the center's core in America is occupied by the poor, whose ranks are swelled by Negro and Puerto Rican migrants.

Growth patterns in America also have interesting parallelisms in the history of Europe. For example, Holland's sixteenth-century growth was focused primarily in the countryside and in the same small city; it was not till after 1575 that centers like Amsterdam, Leiden, Haarlem, Delft, and Rotterdam began to expand. Similarly in the United States our early population growths were in the countryside and small cities, and it was not until the current century that this pattern was significantly reversed. It is too speculative to dwell on that aspect of American city development which has seen a decline in numbers in the city proper, but it is a fact that American cities have had periods of rapid population growth followed by slow declines. Causes of the decline are not known, but the relationship of city growth to general economic prosperity seems very clear.

One remarkable characteristic of western Europe is this: everywhere west of a straight line running from St. Petersburg down through Trieste, the marriage age for women was high until very recent times. In contrast, in most other parts of the world, women married at much earlier ages, and nearly all women married. In western Europe many men and women never married, with the result that a typical family unit included servants and unmarried relatives. The important consequences of this pattern was marked lowering of fertility and of the capability in western Europe to respond quickly to changes in the general economy. Fewer jobs meant fewer children. While Americans may tend to follow this delayed-marriage pattern, but the postwar period has brought a sharp reversal, with consequent complications for urban growth.

DEFINITIONS AND IDEOLOGIES

The tremendous explosion of populations in urban areas is creating serious problems of definition. Is a city the area defined by its legal boundaries or by the number of persons who earn their livelihood within its borders? Is a city simply the central core? Or is it the nucleus for all those satellite communities revolving about it and held in some special orbit by the magnetic pull of the center? Or is a contemporary city a "nonplace"?

The problem is neatly illustrated by the United States of 2000 for which have been projected three tremendous population centers: "Boswash," "Chipitz," and "SanSan," respectively.[7] The first refers to a 500-mile stretch running from Boston to Washington, which will include eighty million people, or one-quarter of the nation's total population. "Chipitz," a megalopolis concentrated around the Great Lakes, will extend from Chicago to Pittsburgh and will provide homes for over forty million people—about 12 per cent of the nation's population. "SanSan" denotes the Pacific complex that will stretch from San Francisco to Santa Barbara with a population of some twenty million Americans. Within these three areas will live approximately half the United States population which, in turn, includes the overwhelming majority of the country's most technological and scientifically advanced individuals and the society's most prosperous and most creative elements. SanSan, smallest of the three units, will have a larger total income than all but five or six nations of the world.

Fantastic as are projections for the United States, they do not equal the prophecies made by some scholars for Japan. Indeed, in some respects, Tokyo itself may provide a prototype for the future *international* city. At present the city's twenty-three wards and tama-guns (the centers of administrative convenience) include a population of approximately nine million people. If, however, one defines Tokyo as the area wherein people earn their living, it becomes necessary to extend what is called Tokyo-To to a fifty-kilometer circle from the center, to include Kanagawa, Saitama, and Chiba. Today this population is over twenty-two million and if this becomes the unit upon which projections are made, the metropolitan population may exceed the one-hundred million mark by 2000. The implication of this kind of growth is of special relevance because Japan herself is a developed area surrounded by other underdeveloped societies.[8]

Clearly, then, any tendency to define a city by its legal boundaries alone produces a conception often unrelated to reality. In the United States, for example, there were only ten cities in 1910 which had a population of over one million; in 1960 there were sixty-one cities in this category. Yet in the decade following 1950 all except one of the ten largest cities lost population even as the urban areas continued to grow.[9] The apparent contradiction is the result of different definitions of the city—descriptions that may overemphasize our affluence to the neglect of our "effluence."[10] It is the affluent society that explains how population in the suburban areas increased five times faster than in the central cities and why, between 1950 and 1960, more than three-fourths of metropolitan growth occurred outside the central areas. Indeed in a single decade (1950-1960) metropolitan "colonies" outside the central cities increased their population by 61.7 per cent, whereas central cities showed a population growth of only 1.5 per cent.[11] But numbers are not the only problem; there are other categories for viewing a city and Professor Abrams of Columbia expressed the issue in these terms:[12]

American cities embrace a variety of categories. They are large and small, trade centers and industrial centers, rich and poor. They are as heterogeneous as the people who inhabit them. In assessing the state and fate of American cities, one should distinguish between polymorphic cities like New York or Chicago, and cities like Gary, Detroit, Grand Rapids, or Fall River, that all their lives may lean to one or two industries and might die with their departure. There are American capital cities that never change anything but their governors, cities that are no more than languid milltowns, cities that have more houses than people, cities dominated by the aging, cities with most of their houses on wheels, cities like Los Angeles that spread for miles and are still spreading, and one city in California that supports its quick from the burial fees of its dead.

Awareness of these differences prompted one of our essayists, Constantinos Doxiadis, to suggest that we forget the word "city" and concentrate on the term "human settlement." One could then predict a continuation of migration toward the metropolitan areas, which would produce what he terms an *ecumenopolis*—the system of living in interconnected cities which constitute, in turn, one huge "universal city." If the ecumenopolis is the ultimate in urban development, the challenge is to make this center a place fit for human survival and human growth.

As twentieth-century man works toward this universal city he remains conscious of the intermediate stages and knows that wherever he lives and by whatever name it is called—a metropolis,[13] a megalopolis,[14] or urban realm[15]—problems of definition are less important than problems arising from human dissatisfactions. Perhaps President Johnson, in a footnote to his message to Congress on March 2, 1965, provided the most practical definition when he described the city as "the entire urban area—the central city and its suburbs." And the cardinal role to be played by future cities was captured by the President in a commencement address at the University of Michigan in 1964 when he declared: "The great society is where the city of man serves not only the needs of the body and the demands of commerce, but the desire for beauty and the hunger for community."[16] The Chief Executive's enthusiasm for the city recalls the view of his illustrious namesake, Dr. Samuel Johnson, who declared: "To be tired of London is to be tired of life!"

Despite current interest in the city, there have been in America dissenters from Dr. Johnson's view who have exercised a rather profound influence on the value climate of our society. Inspired by Jefferson, these rural utopians claim that the city represents a threat to those fundamental values that made America great. It was the view of eighteenth-century London and Paris as dirty and sordid that led Jefferson to work diligently to have Congress approve the so-called "Residence Bill" of July 1796.[17] The primary motive was to get the nation's capital out of "dangerous" New York, then the country's true vital center, even if it meant locating in an unpromising swampland along the Potomac.

This bias may explain why cities have had such difficult times raising money to meet burgeoning local needs and why urban school systems are in a state of such sad repair. Regarding urban education, perhaps a typical view was expressed by the Commissioner of Agriculture in 1866, who declared that "in the formation of a national education, as of a national character, the country more than the city must control. As the city becomes more cosmopolitan, its people . . . lose distinctive characteristics, and, judging from popular manifestations, love of country as well. Ignorance concentrates and while the favored few enjoy superior facilities and attain scholarly reputation in surpassing most people in the country, they are but the few, and the proportion which can never exist in the country are doomed to ignorance unillumined by any sign of amelioration."[18] Contemplating the inroads of urbanization, Thoreau at an earlier date concluded that he could no longer rest comfortable amidst the nervous, bustling and trivial world of the nineteenth century and that he must "stand or sit thoughtfully while it goes by!"[19] But for everyone who, with Thoreau, was content to "step aside" there were five others who identified the city as their place for economic advancement and greater security or, at least, so they thought. This enormous appeal was heavily economic in nature and meant that business played a substantial role in the cities' development and evolution.

AMERICAN BUSINESS AND THE AMERICAN CITY

It is abundantly clear from our survey that urban growth is correlated to the general economic level of the community and that business, therefore, has a crucial role to play. If this is true, can business find comfort or derive sorrow from the present situation that describes the contemporary American society? The growth of the American community sheds fascinating light on the old debate be-between (a) those who argue that cities grow naturally because of their physical advantages and (b) those who hold that creative leadership constitutes the significant difference because it plans deliberately for urban development.

It is well known, of course, that before the Civil War an intense rivalry for trade existed among New York, Philadelphia, and Baltimore. Prior to the opening of the Erie Canal trade to the West was carried on chiefly by Baltimore and Philadelphia, and particularly by the latter which was at the time the first city of the United States in population, wealth, and the amount of internal commerce. But a significant element needs to be remarked upon and Charles N. Glaab described that element in these terms:[20]

> In retrospect it is easy to explain New York's rise to metropolitan dominance in terms of its superior natural advantages—a magnificent harbor, for example, or the reasonably level terrain westward across New York State which permitted the Erie Canal to be built with relative ease. It is also possible to point to organizational and entrepreneurial actions on the part of the city's business community that earlier help to insure the city's success.

These successful programs included: (1) obtaining of the passage of favorable auction laws; (2) organization of regular liner service to England; and (3) successful development of the coastal trade, particularly in bringing cotton from the South. The Erie Canal, completed in 1825, greatly accelerated the city's rise. The spectacular success of the Canal stimulated New York's rivals (Boston, Philadelphia, and Baltimore) toward efforts to compete more effectively, and the responses reflected not so much differences in geographical and technological circumstances, but rather differences within the business elites of the three communities.

Baltimore merchant leaders, demonstrating a characteristic boldness, endorsed a then unproven transportation innovation to launch in 1828 construction of the Baltimore & Ohio Railroad. The state of Pennsylvania, at Philadelphia's urging, spent approximately $14 million on a 395-mile "Main Line" connection between Philadelphia and Pittsburgh, which combined canal and railroad in a highly unsatisfactory system. The Main Line never proved a formidable rival of the Erie, and in a few years it had become clear that Philadelphia should have supported a railroad. If Philadelphia suffered reverses, so did Boston. In 1868 the distinguished Charles Francis Adams, Jr. noted the stranglehold Boston once had on the Liverpool trade; entrepreneurship and innovation in Liverpool kept that city from being submerged under London's leadership, whereas a lack of leadership saw the gradual shift in trade from Boston to New York.

In mid-America a rivalry somewhat similar to the Philadelphia-New York contest characterized relationships between St. Louis and Chicago. Again, it was Adams who wrote that in 1837 Chicago was perhaps the deadest place in the whole broad land. The city was bankrupt; the state was bankrupt; work on the canal and railroads was suspended. By 1850, however, the city boasted a population of 30,000 inhabitants and a railroad system comprising forty-two miles, all in successful operation. "Thus a young city of the west has distinctively appreciated the position and necessity of the country and of the ages; she has flung herself, heart, soul, and body into the movement of her times; she has realized a great fact that steam has revolutionized the world, and she had bound her whole existence up in the great power of modern times. But for this, St. Louis might well have proved to her what New York has proved to Boston."[21] In one sense St. Louis business leaders seem to have demonstrated a reluctance to take big risks and to pursue those bold policies of business expansion and urban growth which their Chicago counterparts embarked upon so eagerly.

It is this concern with creative leadership that possibly induced Margaret Mead to identify specifically in her essay the remarkable success of Corning, New York. Populated by 17,000 people, this relatively small community along the Chemung River will soon celebrate its 200th anniversary. A key element in the city's success has been the family-owned and family-managed Corning Glass Works. The same skill and innovation that went into successful business management were deployed effectively towards urban management. As a consequence, notes Dr. Mead, Corning has today one of the finest school systems in New York, excellent hospital facilities, a library that services over 100,000 people living in the Chemung Valley area, a philharmonic orchestra, and the Corning Glass Center that attracts creative people from all over the world.

At the same time, one is drawn inexorably to note that creative leadership must be adaptive to changes in the physical and economic order. Henry A. Miles described Lowell, Massachusetts, as a city which, between 1826 and 1836, once "laid broad and deep the foundations of a great community. New streets were opened, houses and stores were put up, churches were erected, canals were dug, manufacturing operations were extended, and within this ten-year span the population of the town was multiplied sixfold. This increase was without parallel in any place and in any country. This prosperity was the result of the sagacity, enterprise, and energy of the capitalists and manufacturers by whom the fortunes of the town were guided."[22]

But the determination of its founder, Francis Cabot Lowell, to establish a paternalistic corporate community designed to realize the noble dream of a good Christian life was eroding even at the very time that Miles wrote his panegyric. Competition from other factories powered by coal, good profit from real-estate speculation, and the steady stream of newly arrived immigrants to swell the labor force resulted in a rapid decline for Lowell. Corning and Lowell underscore the danger of relying too much on "historic" performance of the business or political community as a guarantor of future success. History is instructive, but in today's world each new day brings new challenges. These challenges are enormous indeed and can be only illustrated by an examination of the present state of the city. If business has often helped and sometimes hindered sensible urban growth in the past, what prospects exist for the future?

THE CONTEMPORARY AMERICAN CITY:
PATHOLOGY OR PROFILE?

One of the most notable and less desirable features of business was the desire to speculate in land. Compulsion to parcel out land quickly so as to make speculative sales resulted in the building lot becoming the fundamental unit of measure. This speculative building lot was such a small unit that it resulted in an inorganic type of layout. But even today the builder of tracts, who has a real chance to confer some uniformity on the land, thinks basically in terms of the number of lots he can subdivide. The city was chopped into a rectangular gridiron shape and pieces sold quickly. The land interest was soon replaced by, or converted to, money interest, and the layout and building of the city was done with little regard to its topographical characteristics, prevailing winds, soil conditions, or relationships to other industries.

Unlike Europe whose cities had learned to control layout, the American city grew like Topsy and the orthodox gridiron became, at times, a severe handicap to sensible evolution. This helps to explain why San Francisco has streets running up steep hills and why New York has streets which funnel the wind.

Another aspect of business impact was the construction of buildings that were utilitarian, functional in design, and simple to replace. Land prices within the city grew sharply and the result was predictable: not only was there horizontal expansion because of the gridiron pattern but there was also vertical expansion in the form of skyscrapers. Large apartment blocks arose and profits were maximized through high rents, cost cutting, and reduction in services. One could scarcely be surprised at the subsequent ease whereby these apartment blocks could degenerate into slum dwellings. Apartments were so crowded that streets became playgrounds. This concern prompted the New York Chapter of the American Institute of Architects to declare that "the field of speculative and investment architecture requires much more serious consideration than it received. And that New York is not getting benefits commensurate with the money, energy and effort that are going into its development."[23]

Under the dominant market ideology of the late nineteenth century, railroads, driven into the heart of the city, dissected living quarters, spread soot and dirt, and abetted the formation of noisy and bulky industries. In the process of searching for the private good, the public interest was not infrequently jettisoned. As Paul N. Ylvisaker

14

observed: "We divided the city into pieces, let it become a jungle of competing objectives and conflicting codes of ethics, and then blithely assumed that by some undefined process our several self-interests would add up to the common benefit."[24]

If business seriously affects the physical contours of the city, it can also create enormous problems of traffic flow within buildings, even when they are aesthetically attractive. The new Pan-Am Building over the Grand Central Station in New York, for example, reportedly houses over 25,000 employees and congestion at rush hours is enormous. Additionally, business firms require huge amounts of materials and supplies. With the development of trucking, plant location is less dependent on railroads for movement of goods. The result is that the truck has become the dominant transport mechanism within the city center; loading facilities are often inadequate and the lines upon lines of trucks disgorging their ware or taking on commodities add to the noise and congestion of city streets.

What are the results? One answer comes from August Heckscher, who says that "the journey to work is enough to unfit the individual for anything genuinely free or creative; a day spent in the city is not devoted to most of those influences which refreshen and liven the spirit."[25] The urban scene is one of pandemonium, of nerve-wracking tension, of sound and fury, of high-powered vehicles moving at snail-like speeds. Rather than dwell on the multiple aspects of the city problems, it may prove illustrative to concentrate on one, pollution, which is often blamed on business. It should be emphasized that while the following notations are intended purely for illustrative purposes they do show why business is often the object of sharp rebuke.

POLLUTION AS A TYPICAL URBAN PROBLEM

Consolidated Edison in New York has felt the lash most painfully in recent years because it operates 116 boilers and fifty smokestacks in the metropolitan area. Pollution is, of course, not an altogether new phenomenon. Approximately seventy-five years ago Sir Edwin Chadwick, disturbed by the great blankets of fog over London, proposed the formation of a "Pure Air Company" to draw air from a suitable height and distribute it into the houses—and to do it with a profit at a very low rate.[26] Even earlier the poet Shelley had written: "Hell is a city much like London, a populous and a smoky city." And if one wants to employ the historical game even further one may recall that 2,000 years earlier Seneca talked of the stench of city chimneys in Rome.

Over New York City alone pours each year approximately 230,000 tons of soot, 597,000 tons of sulphur dioxide, 298,000 tons of nitrogen oxide, 567,000 tons of hydrocarbons, and 1,536,000 tons of carbon monoxide. In a biting satire on New York as the "fume city," Dick Schaap wrote in the *New York Magazine* (April 15, 1968) this comment:

> Beyond its natural loveliness, pollution serves the city of New York in so many ways. It helps keep the City from becoming overpopulated; it insures that only the fittest survive and the rest move to the suburbs. It helps keep the City from becoming overgrown with foliage; it kills roses and tulips and other harmful weeds. It provides enjoyment for window washers and car-washers and eager little shoe-shine boys. And it saves money: it provides all the joys of cigarette smoking without any of the expenses.

From Schaap's satire, the "beauty part" of air pollution is that it is for all the people: it discriminates neither by race or religion, age or sex, rich or poor; the air in New York provides each individual with 700 pounds of pollution each year and is an inalienable right: "it is like a good view of a good mugging, one of the fringe benefits of city living."

Satire is one route that some take to dramatize the problems. The majority of critics are more somber in the tenor of their criticisms. The President's Science Advisory Committee, for one, declared that there exists no right to pollute, that the public must learn to recognize individual rights to a quality of living as expressed by the absence of pollution as it has come to recognize the rights to education, to economic advancement, and to public recreation. Yet the clamor is scarcely strident, despite the publicity given to the tragedy in Donora, Pennsylvania, and in London when the "black fog" of December 1952 accounted for over 4,000 deaths. Inaction is surprising because those who have studied air pollution tend to agree with Geoffrey Dean who declared that, in the light of evidence he had collected in New Zealand, South Africa, Australia, and the Channel Islands, it seemed most reasonable to conclude that there is an association between urbanization and lung cancer.

Because motor vehicles account for approximately 60 per cent of the air pollution, it is argued that the automobile industry has failed us miserably.[27] And a "black eye" for one industry or one firm is often a bruise for all business. We are told that if the automobile firms would install such devices as direct flame after-burners we could remove up to 80 per cent of carbon monoxide and hydrocarbons from crank-case and exhaust emissions. In fact it has been recommended that the future cities be divided into two layers where automobiles would operate through tunnels from which the air would be rapidly pumped and treated to remove obnoxious substances, and people would walk on the higher level.[28]

Water pollution is just as serious. In the so-called "Penjerdel Region" (Trenton, Philadelphia, and the Wilmington metropolitan areas) industrial waste materials flowing into the Delaware River have a density equivalent to that of the sewage of over 2.6 million people. One-fourth of this material is removed by treatment, but three-quarters (equivalent to a population of 1.9 million people) is discharged into the Delaware. The story is in sorry contrast to the business-government performance in the Ruhr River Basin which contains the heaviest industrial concentration of Western Germany. Operating under the Ruhr Valley Administration, the Ruhr River system is used and reused eight times over and still remains clean enough for fishing and swimming.

It is, therefore, quite clear that American business has a significant role to play in offsetting this one aspect of deteriorating urban life. Other aspects could be cited where business has a key role to perform. It is important to recall that when the *Report of the National Advisory Committee on Civil Disorders* listed first-, second-, and third-order of causes of rioting, among the first-order causes were housing needs and

17

unemployment.[29] Areas for possible responses by the business community will be noted shortly and discussed in some detail in the concluding chapter. It is sufficient to note here that success in dealing with the problems of urban America are heavily dependent on business performance.

THE CONTEMPORARY CORPORATION AND THE CITY

At this juncture it is relevant to review the nature of the modern American corporation and to inquire, from a *theoretical* standpoint, whether or not the corporation can make a significant contribution to the contemporary urban crisis. Surely the desire is there. For example, Andrew Heiskell of the Urban Coalition and Board Chairman of *Time Incorporated* noted that businessmen must act—and quickly—because cities are in deep trouble. Said Mr. Heiskell:[30]

We can already see signs of erosion; you can see signs of erosion when a telephone man refuses to make repairs in the ghetto unless he is protected by another man. You can see it with teachers when they won't go back to school without police protection. We saw it in Detroit when the firemen had to be protected not only by the police, but by the National Guard.

But if the corporation is to respond in terms of strength, then executives may have to contemplate transforming the corporation into an essentially different instrument than it is now—even as the modern corporation as a social institution has undergone profound changes since World War II. Whatever corporate structural and procedural alterations are made, its ultimate end tends to be one definable in terms of political economy. As an economic institution its role in society is the producing and distributing of wealth. But if one digs into antiquity one discovers that the concept of the corporation is capable of large refinements so that men in voluntary associations can achieve a multiplicity of social goals. More often than not these goals have been tied together, but not so as to subject corporate bodies to the complete mastery of the sovereign state—a purely modern social invention—but rather to make these entities serve man's dominant purposes at the time.[31] The ancient Roman *collegia* and *universitates,* for example, although they were essentially public-sector entities, could serve the function of persons associated in trade in much the same way that *collegia* and the medieval guilds served both business and other social purposes. And in the history of corporations no "bodies corporate and politic" were more important than incorporated towns and cities.

The limited-liability features of modern companies, on the other hand, have their legal roots in the medieval conception of the "corporate person," an extremely useful fiction which serves not only the business community but society generally. Universities, churches, cultural institutions, and a wide range of other organized activities likewise make use of the well-nigh indispensable *persona ficta*—an essentially political concept that leads logically to the idea of social responsibility because corporate personality derives (at least in American jurisprudence) from a public act. And it is widely assumed that all incorporated bodies enjoy a privilege that the sovereign alone can bestow.

The modern corporation, however, whether it be a business or a nonprofit entity, is by no means content to let matters stand there. A corporation is an instrument of the state in only a limited sense. It is more realistically an instrument of society, and in a democratic society it is a means of achieving man's human and humane goals. That is why, in a free society, so much emphasis is put upon freedom of association, including the freedom to incorporate, and upon home rule for cities. In both cases, man seeks liberation from the extensive grasp of sovereign states whose central political bodies and administrative agencies are often viewed as threats to man's civilizing activities. Business has always been a major advocate of the principle of freedom of enterprise to ward off the oppressive sovereign.

But corporations can themselves become private rulers of a subtler sort. This raises more than the banal question about the "Organization Man." It raises the question of broad corporate objectives, and in the present case, of corporate objectives that may or may not run parallel to, and complementary of, the civilized goals of urban life.

At this point we must ask what those who direct the affairs of the modern corporation believe to be their relationship to contemporary and future urban civilization, and how corporate objectives and company policies need to be drawn to serve man's purposes in that civilization. We have seen that business institutions have always been influenced by their social environment, as they have often influenced that environment, for both good and ill. The modern corporation, in particular, although the subject of frequent attack, survives as a dominant business institution, however, because it is so advantageous an instrument. Nor is it the instrument alone of its security-holders. Those who buy its products and services, those who sell their products and services to it, those on whom its activities impinge—all look to it as an instrument. To public governments, the modern corporation is not only a big taxpayer; it is also a big supplier of goods and services during war and in peace. But domestic peace is disturbed by urban crisis and the corporation has a new challenge.

To meet this challenge, of course, means that the corporation must change with the times. There are many who deny that it can change or ought to "stray" beyond strictly industrial, commercial, and entrepreneurial activities. But as some of its expositors have already made abundantly clear, the evidence is against this line of argument for the mature corporation. In the business world there will continue to be large numbers of relatively small units devoted to traditionally limited "business" activities. Ventures and wild-catting will proceed apace wherever vast opportunities exist. But the largest business organizations are already institutionalized instruments of society for many kinds of social functions, and this trend will hardly be reversed. The direction is toward what is often called social responsibilities.

The trouble with talking about social responsibilities of business is that the talk is so generalized and vague.

Every person and organization has duties as well as rights, and obligations that must be met in any civilized society. The more useful approach to the corporate role in cities is an ecological one. What we need to know is the urban matrix of successful business, the specific characteristics and forces of the ecosystem in densely populated urban centers and in metropolitan areas that sustain corporate life. In reverse, the expository problem is the role of corporations in a balanced eco-system (local, national, regional, multinational, conceived in modern terms of outer and oceanic space) that serves man as a free agent of human dignity.

Once the place of the modern corporation is thus understood in its social and spatial context, there will be an appropriate time to expound the responsibilities of persons and organizations on all sides. Until these things are understood and there is agreement on goals for man, it will be premature to dogmatize on the role of corporations and cities in civilization. That some progress is being made in business circles toward an ecological study of the corporation in these terms, and with special reference to urban problems, is a good sign that we are at least on our way. It is equally evident that we still have a long way to go.

In the midst of the urban crisis of the late 'sixties, a spokesman for the life insurance companies of América published a parable that indicates the depth of the problem and the corporate stake in its solu-tion. The parable referred to a huge dam built at the foot of Mt. Toc in northern Italy. In the valley below lay the town of Longarone. Some of the residents of Longarone tried to have the project halted because the mountains around the dam had a bad history of avalanches. Nobody much listened. The dam was built. One day earth began falling into the lake behind the dam. Some of the residents became alarmed. But no one did anything about it. Then one night, when everyone was asleep or watching a soccer match on TV, a huge chunk of earth fell from Mt. Toc sending a 300-foot wall of water crashing over the dam. In a matter of minutes, Longarone disappeared from the face of the earth.

The state of our cities was compared with Longarone. We were aware of the strains that threaten urban life, yet the warnings were not heeded. The cities' cracks and strains were showing in the slums, in the jobless, in the crime rate, in our polluted air, in our foul rivers and harbors and lakes, and in our roads strangled with traffic. Unless something was done soon, our cities would become giant Longarones. There was still time to avoid greater personal tragedy and the dire economic consequences of failure to act. The paradox was that the very cities suffering under the cracks and strains had the richest human and economic resources in the world.

Yet, therein lay the hope that prevention measures could be taken. What could business and industry do? The job of rehabilitating the cities has to rest primarily with government. But it is too big a job for government alone. It is everybody's problem—business, labor, private citizens, Negro and white alike. Help is needed in building and improving housing, creating job-training centers, re-evaluating hiring practices, participating in community programs of health and education. The Institute of Life Insurance statement has cited cases. Industrial and business leaders have launched a massive drive in Kansas City to hire at least 1,000 hard-core unemployed; in cooperation, the Urban League had scheduled a Career Fair to make jobs available to persons wanting them. A large pharmaceutical company, in cooperation with the Philadelphia Housing Authority, has subsidized partial costs of neighborhood rehabilitation and contributed $26,000 for local job training and information centers. A steel company in Chicago had arranged for one of its Negro personnel executives to appear on a weekly TV program, "Opportunity Line," in a show that broadcast job openings and scheduled interviews for job placement; in the first five weeks, 3,000 people had been placed and calls averaged 2,000 a week. Other companies were helping to build new plants that would train and employ disadvantaged people.

A group of life insurance companies had made a commitment to invest one billion dollars for housing and jobs in slum areas, nearly half of which had already been earmarked for specific projects. Businesses throughout the country were taking up the call to action. But only a beginning had been made. The call went out for collaboration from all sides, including the voluntary work of people everywhere as individuals in citizens' organizations, working with local educational and planning boards, and lending their support to community efforts to meet the problem. The cities had now become one of the greatest challenges the country had ever faced. It was everybody's crisis. But business itself had joined the war on urban ills on a scale that was new. The evidence of this was to be seen in the Urban Coalition.

THE URBAN COALITION

The Urban Coalition was launched in the summer of 1967 soon after the riots in Newark and Detroit, but the idea had germinated in the fall of 1966 when mayors sensed grave disorders in the offing. Leaders from five major segments of American society responded: business, labor, religion, racial minorities, and local government. In March 1968, John W. Gardner, who had recently resigned his cabinet post as Secretary of Health, Education, and Welfare, became the national chairman of the Urban Coalition, a full-time job. The drive to raise up the cities' "ghettos" had several phases: more money for the war on poverty, more money for summer jobs for ghetto youth, more public housing and rent supplements, and support for the open housing bill then before Congress. The Coalition was against a freeze on welfare payments that Congress had enacted the year before. It asked the government to provide "public service jobs" for those of the unemployed who could find no jobs in private industry. A big price tag was put on those public service jobs, at least $4 billion. The Coalition's first convocation in August 1967 drew 1,200 community leaders who, according to Whitney Young, executive director of the National Urban League, had "enough power to turn this country around." It was a coalition that provided businessmen with a forum for more than an exchange of ideas in the face of ominous threats; it committed them to a direct confrontation with ghetto and racial problems in the nation's cities and to a serious attempt to hammer out practicable programs with Negro leaders and the leaders of other major segments of society. The question was whether this method would succeed.

The Urban Coalition was not to be limited to a national forum. Coalitions were to be found in at least 100 major cities. At the local level attempts would be made to mobilize a broad base of community support for jobs, housing, schools, and other programs. Task forces at both national and local levels were assigned to these specific problems, chiefly to act as catalyzers for new programs but also to organize some themselves. The Ford Foundation helped to support the first year's $3 million budget for the National Urban Coalition, and funds were sought from business, labor, and religious groups for both national and local coalitions. At the first national convocation in 1967 there was a call for "a major expansion of private-sector programs to provide jobs and training for the hard-core poor." Soon thereafter Henry Ford II, a coalition member, became chairman of the newly founded National Alliance of Businessmen; this alliance, backed by $350 million in government funds, set for itself the task of persuading business to put 100,000 hard-core slum residents into special education and training programs.

Critics of this coalition approach to urban problems predicted failure. Private-sector leaders, it was said, would not be able to marshal the required human and financial resources to make a real dent, nor would they support the necessary public expenditures (and tax increases) to assure the necessary public-sector programs. The Urban Coalition did, however, demonstrate that leaders of business, labor, civil rights organizations, and churches could collaborate with mayors more effectively than any such groupings had done before. That the coalition would achieve only part of the task posed by the urban crisis of our age would be no mark against it. The problem is of too vast a scale to merit that kind of criticism.

Richard Eells and Clarence Walton

OTHER EFFORTS

Other forces and other organizations in the business community were needed and many are now at work. Prominent among them are the National Industrial Conference Board and the Committee for Economic Development (CED). CED was established after World War II to help in the change-over from wartime production and controls to peacetime competition and growth. CED promoted the discussion of new ideas, policies, and programs, particularly proposals for countering the expected postwar recession that did not in fact occur but was widely feared at home and abroad at the time. CED is composed of two hundred leading businessmen and educators. Its basic objectives are: (1) to develop, through objective research and discussion, findings and recommendations for business and public policy which will contribute to the preservation and strengthening of our free society, and to the maintenance of high employment, increasing productivity and living standards, greater economic stability, and greater opportunity for all our people; and (2) to bring about increasing public understanding of the importance of these objectives and the ways in which they can be achieved.

CED's work is supported by voluntary contributions from business and industry. It is nonprofit, nonpartisan, and nonpolitical. The trustees, who generally are presidents or board chairmen of corporations and presidents of universities, are chosen for their individual capacities rather than as representatives of any particular interests. They unite scholarship with business judgment and experience in analyzing the issues and developing recommendations to resolve the economic problems that constantly arise in a dynamic and democratic society.

Through this business-academic partnership, CED endeavors to develop policy statements and other research products that commend themselves as guides to public and business policy; for use as texts in college economic and political science courses and in management

25

training courses; for consideration and discussion by newspaper and magazine editors, columnists and commentators; and for distribution abroad to promote better understanding of the American economic system.

CED believes that by enabling businessmen to demonstrate constructively their concern for the general welfare, it is helping business to earn and maintain the national and community respect essential to the successful functioning of the free enterprise capitalist system.

In practice, CED's research goes into some of the most important areas of corporate ecology—including problems of local government that affect today's urban crisis. Its Area Development Committee, for example, had already in 1959 issued studies of the metropolis and the central city.[32] Recognizing the urgent need for improvement in governmental structures and processes at all levels, CED's research and policy committees have issued studies on modernizing state and local governments and on the improvement of government management at the national level as well.[33] CED's influence extends beyond the impact of these published studies. In the continuous involvement of its members in public problems, the organization brings to bear on the urban crisis executive action that is backed by scholarly thought as well as judgment based on research and clash of mind in the policy committees.

In these and other ways the corporate sector of the business community has begun to move to meet problems of the city. If business has contributed to a city's ills, it must contribute to a city's recovery. If it has nourished the city in the past, it can sustain it even more over the long-term future. The following essays by world-renowned experts give some realistic interpretations of the challenge and the opportunity.

Richard Eells and *Clarence Walton*

NOTES

1. Lewis Mumford, "Utopia, the City, and the Machine," *Daedalus* (Spring 1965), p. 271.

2. Lewis Mumford, *The City in History* (New York: Harcourt, Brace & World Inc., 1961), pp. 81-100.

3. Mumford, *op. cit.*, p. 100.

4. Gerald Sykes, *The Cool Millennium* (Englewood Cliffs, N. J., Prentice-Hall Inc., 1967), Chapter 2.

5. Quoted in Clarence C. Walton "Critics of Business: Stonethrowers and Gravediggers" *Columbia Journal of World Business* (Fall 1966), pp. 25-37.

6. Lord Bryce, *Modern Democracies*, I (New York, The Macmillan Company, 1961), p. 108.

7. Herman Kahn and Anthony J. Wiener, *The Year 2000* (New York: The Macmillan Company, 1968), p. 61.

8. These implications are explored by Masatoshi Matsushiti in his essay "Tokyo in 2000 A.D.," which is included in this collection.

9. George Sternlieb, "Is Business Abandoning the Big City?" *Harvard Business Review*, XXXIX (January-February 1961), p. 7.

10. This intriguing coinage of terms was made by Charles A. Abrams in *The City Is the Frontier* (New York: Harper & Row, 1965), pp. 8-12.

11. Warren J. Winton, "The Census of 1960," *Housing Year-Book* (National Housing Conference, 1961), p. 2.

12. Abrams, *op. cit.*, p. 6.

13. Raymond Vernon, *Metropolis 1985* (New York: Doubleday & Co., 1963), p. 24.

14. Jean Gottman, *Megalopolis* (New York: The Twentieth Century Fund, 1961), p. 3.

15. Melvin L. Webber, *The Urban Place and Urban Non-Place* (Philadelphia: University of Pennsylvania Press, 1964).

16. "United States Cities: A Surge of New Life," *Business Week* (July 4, 1964), p. 11.

17. James Young, *The Washington Community 1800-1828* (New York: Columbia University Press, 1966), p. 16.

18. Quoted in Charles E. Glaab, *The American City: A Documentary History* (Homewood, Illinois: The Dorsey Press, Inc., 1963), pp. 6-23.

19. Leo Marx, *The Machine in the Garden* (New York: Oxford University Press, 1964), p. 265.

20. Glaab, *op. cit.*, pp. 66-67.

21. Charles F. Adams, Jr., "Boston," *North American Review*, CVI (January 1968), as quoted in Glaab, *op. cit.*, pp. 192-193.

22. Glaab, *op. cit.*, p. 143.

23. Richard Whelan, "The City Destroying Itself," *Fortune*, LXX (September 1964), p. 116.

24. "The Miraculous City," *National Civic Review*, I (December 1961), p. 590.

25. August Heckscher, "The City and the Human Being," in Clarence C. Walton, ed., *Today's Changing Society: The Challenge to Individual Identity* (New York: Institute of Life Insurance Co., 1967), p. 76.

26. B. Ward, "Sir Edwin Chadwick," *National Health* (London, 1890), p. 311.

27. Power plants contribute another 15 per cent to air pollution and industry generally contributes about 17 per cent. Space heating and refuse disposal account for approximately 9 per cent. See Abel Wolman, "Air Pollution: Time for Appraisal," *Science*, March 29, 1968, p. 1347.

28. Roger Revelle, "Pollution in Cities," in James Wilson, ed. *The Metropolitan Enigma* (Washington: U. S. Chamber of Commerce, 1967), pp. 78-123.

29. See the *U. S. Riot Commission Report* (New York: The New York Times Co., 1968), particularly Chapter 17.

30. Andrew Heiskell, "The Arithmetic of the City," *Public Relations Journal,* XXIV, January, 1968, p. 25.

31. Selections from Schumpeter, Rostovtzeff, Beard, Jarrett, Sombart, Gierke, and others, in C. Walton and R. Eells, eds., *The Business System: Readings in Ideas and Concepts,* I (New York: The Macmillan Company, 1967), Vol. I, Part 1.

32. Raymond Vernon, *The Changing Economic Function of the Central City* (New York: Committee for Economic Development, 1959); and Robert C. Wood, *Metropolis Against Itself* (New York: Committee for Economic Development, 1959). Other CED statements and supplementary papers include: *Developing Metropolitan Transportation Policies: A Guide for Local Leadership* (1965); *Distressed Areas in a Growing Economy* (1961); *Guiding Metropolitan Growth* (1960); *Community Economic Development Efforts: Five Case Studies* (1964); *How a Region Grows* (1963); Charles M. Tiebout, *The Community Economic Base Study* (1962); and Donald R. Gilmore, *Developing the Little Economies: A Survey of Area Development Programs in the United States* (1960).

33. Among these CED publications are: *Modernizing Local Government to Secure a Balanced Federalism* (1966); *Modernizing State Government* (1967); *A Fiscal Program for a Balanced Federalism* (1967); *Budgeting for National Objectives* (1966); *Presidential Succession and Inability* (1965); and *Improving Executive Management in the Federal Government* (1964).

2

Margaret Mead

The Crucial Role of the Small City in Meeting the Urban Crisis

The world faces a crisis in building shelter for its burgeoning billions and in designing towns and cities within which they can live safe, healthy, and rewarding lives. We will have to build, within the next twenty-five years, as many more units of shelter as there are now in existence. And most of the housing in the world is obsolete, unsafe, unsanitary, deteriorated, uneconomic, and unlovely. Only the most vigorous international and national efforts will make it possible for us to act with sufficient wisdom, to take advantage of all that we already know, and to set up research that will ensure our learning more in time to meet the needs. We will be building millions of houses, re-designing old cities and building new ones. We will be laying down enormous stretches of road, laying out new airports, setting up new factories, building schools and colleges to hold the millions who will be streaming into them. That we will build is certain, but how we will build, whether we will take advantage of this crisis to build wisely and well, is not at all certain. The crisis is only newly recognized in all its depth. It gives us an opportunity that will not come again in this century. Only with concerted efforts at every level, involving industry, government, science, and citizenry, can we hope to accomplish what is necessary.

To meet the great needs we will have to use every device to transform ancient cities with camel tracks or carriage roads too narrow for automobiles, to rehabilitate cities that have recently decayed at the center as the result of the flight of the middle class from the cities and the flight of the rural poor into the cities. We will have to promote the growth of well-located small towns, combine cities which have been independent, build authorities which can combine local government units and work within large areas that cross municipal, state, and national boundaries. We will have to redesign our great conurbations, which stretch out through miles of anonymity and disorganization, into focused, well-organized, responsible, large communities with well-designed neighborhoods where children may be reared and old people live in safety among familiar things. We will have to design and build many kinds of new cities.

In this paper I wish to concentrate on just one of our options—the strengthening of the existing small cities of the world so that they can make their contribution to the solution of the problems presented by urbanization.

The existing small cities provide us with one of our most valuable bases for new development. They occupy choice sites, at natural crossroads and junctions, on rivers, on good harbors, at places where mountains are passable. They were chosen long ago by natural selection for small settlements, some of which grew and flourished while others withered and died. They have sources of water; they have centers. Those who have lived there have chosen appropriate paths and out of the paths roads have grown. Many of the hazards of the completely new city, where planners lack both a living knowledge of the local peculiarities of wind and sun, rain and tempest, and any certainty as to what kind of people will live there, can be avoided in the old cities. A core population is already there; the weight of the snowfall on the house roofs has been tested and known. When the small city grows, it can grow along lines which have already been tested and tried; new buildings can be placed where the old buildings were or placed elsewhere because the old site has been demonstrated to be unsuitable for the motor age. And as in the physical plant, so in the social; there will already exist old established institutions, clubs and associations, schools and banks and insurance companies, lawyers and doctors. In a completely new city all these have to be imported and built from scratch.

There are, of course, disadvantages in old small cities also. Characteristically, the most ambitious people tend to leave small cities for larger cities. Those who remain are often ultraconservative and cautious. The leaders are likely to have stayed because they have inherited wealth and position too tempting to leave; such leaders are not enthusiastic about change. In their wish to maintain control over local conditions they are likely to oppose efforts to bring in more central or national planning and refuse to recognize the need for larger political units to deal with water, air pollution, river and ocean traffic, air traffic, conservation. Newcomers characteristically come from smaller towns and villages with less experience in small city life. Those few who come to small cities from larger cities are likely to be impatient with the slower pace and more old-fashioned ways, and in turn their impatience will be exploited and resented. If the small city is to be redeveloped to play a role in a rapidly expanding and intercommunicating world, these disadvantages must be faced and means must be found to overcome them. It is because of the advantages, because we cannot afford to neglect a single resource, and because it is in small existing cities that service clubs can play the most decisive role, that I have chosen to emphasize the development of existing small cities here.

There are a variety of ways in which the possible contributions, the drawbacks, and the advantages of small cities could be discussed. I shall be speaking in American terms because these are the only ones that I know well and because this meeting is being held in San Juan, which has been influenced by American experience in city planning. But I am also speaking with full recognition that the problems of other countries will be quite different, and sometimes almost diametrically opposite.

As one way of thinking about what can be done with the small city, I want to discuss a model for a new city with a special purpose— that of attracting high-level research institutions. If small cities are to develop new styles and new attractions for high-level institutions and energetic outside leaders, one of the ways of doing so is to develop new emphases, new kinds of industries to replace dying industries, new and distinctive attractions.

BUILDERS OF TOMORROW

In a recent paper delivered to a symposium on "Research and the Community,"[1] I attempted to elaborate a model of an ideal community which would be built up specifically to accommodate a series of research institutions. Such a model can be used as a way of evaluating real communities.

The segregation of those with special interests is an old tradition in the United States in the form of communities of the religiously dedicated, communities of artists, communities in which the political Utopians have experimented. But the community of scientists and technicians specifically concerned with such problems as the development of atomic energy, the instrumental bases of automation, the space sciences, is new—only as old as Oak Ridge, Tennessee. These communities have been heavily influenced by the dictates of security and by the demands imposed by location, on the one hand, and by the desirability of such light, clean, high-level type of industry, on the other. "New electronic industries" has become almost a synonym for "desirable industrial expansion," with the undertone of worry over the dangers of atomic power, fall-out from the location of plants or bases down-wind to urban centers. Association with defense has also created associations with military installations and the special types of isolation and integration peculiar to the military. The problems of public relations for the formation of these new communities are therefore very complex, and the shape such communities take will affect not only the images of the scientist, the engineer, the machine, and the future of human beings, which are held by the surrounding communities, but also those who live in the new technological communities will reflect these views and come to think of themselves in many of the same ways. The image of the scientist and the engineer drawn by school children whose parents are semiliterate conforms in many respects to the image of the scientist presented in the house organs of great engineering firms, or in the advertising pages of *Science* and *The Scientific American*. The feeling that scientific progress may endanger mankind, involve one in treason, destroy precious human relationships, produce unemployment and regimentation—these are all involved in the way in which groups of scientists and engineers and technicians live and relate to other groups in the community.

The special communities of the past—artistic and intellectual, religious or politically utopian—were related to the local ecology; artists and intellectuals have sought communities that were rural or devoted to special pursuits like fishing and have maintained a relationship with the natives which was both close and explicitly different. Utopian communities have almost always included "dignified" manual labor, involving the care of plants and animals. The new technical communities have no such immediate relationships with either the people or the natural life of a region where they work. The location is determined by the availability of power, airports, the presence of other industries and other installations of the same sort. The scientists and engineers are themselves a highly selected group who have developed their special interests in high school, often under counterpressures from family and schoolmates, who welcome isolation from other kinds of people and the relaxation of association with those who speak the same language and have the same detachment from other human beings. The demands they themselves will make on a community and the demands which, in their name and in the name of the state, the nation, and the world, the planners should make for them are often contrasting.

We may expect that the technical group will want good, modern housing, availability of the services which they consider essential, such as accessible airports, shopping centers, good schools, and some sort of recreation for their families. The presence of others who are technically trained will be regarded as an advantage. Space to move around in, freedom from irksome interruptions due to faulty physical planning or tiresome social pressures, ability to get away when they want to— these they will recognize.

As designers, however, there are other needs which they will not recognize as readily but which are urgent if we are to prevent the further fragmentation of knowledge and the development of a technical elite totally out of touch with the humanities, with politics, with the ongoing life of the world. Because of their high intelligence and technical competence, the other steps which must be taken on their behalf must be very high level. Music is the art most likely to appeal to them, and locating a music center or an orchestra in such a community is one way of assuring both a fuller life for the technical group and a diversified human community for themselves and their children. Top technical groups usually contain a few foreigners, and this circumstance can be expanded into specific welcome to intellectual activities related to such institutions as national cultural centers, Casa italiana, international institutes. The technical community should be keyed into circuits of artistic and intellectual resources. There should be a theater to which theatrical companies can come, a documentary film theater, an art gallery for small circulating art collections, a first-class library able to tap both public and private libraries in the state, circulating collections of original paintings, records, tapes of all sorts. In the center of the community there should be services that can tap the

34

whole artistic and intellectual life of the nation efficiently and quickly and without requiring too much "do-it-yourself" of men who work long hours in laboratories.

The scientists and technicians associated with activities of this sort also need an outdoor life provided for them; if the natural world— whether lake, or stream, or forest—is at their door, they will make something of it, if not for themselves then for their children. Community facilities, if the residential areas are diversified, such as swimming pools, shared by adjacent residents, provide for the kind of implicit democracy in the scientific world. The sports they enjoy most are associated with individual skills, and areas in which their children can develop as swimmers, pole vaulters, runners, and so on, are essential, as is provision for tennis, handball, and the like.

All need for activities that involve bringing in groups of lower-status labor, lower-status employees, maintenance men, and so on, should be avoided in favor of designing high-level services and, if necessary, training programs for immigrants. This will involve the residence in the community of highly intelligent but unskilled and possibly illiterate service people, whose children can benefit from the schools and provide some balance to the possible overintellectualization that will be encouraged in the homes of the technical community.

Among scientists and technicians we find a range from those whose primary scientific work is fed by vigorous and enthusiastic activity in many other fields—artistic, athletic, creative—to those who wish to pursue their special interests with absolute single-minded dedication and who regard all other types of activity—mowing the lawn, serving on a committee, going to a concert, or taking the children swimming—as an interruption. There will also be a certain number of married women who are also scientists and technicians and who will parallel this second group of men in their wish to be relieved from the more mundane chores. For the men who wish to work uninterruptedly, and the women who must carry the double or triple responsibilities of a career, wifehood, and motherhood, there is a great need for adequate community services which will relieve a certain section of the homes from domestic drudgery—nursery schools, an organized source of high-level domestic help, gardening and grounds care, inexpensive food services, a repair service that is always accessible.

It is also a mistake to assume that because such communities consist of well-paid and highly trained individuals, there is no need for community social services, such as a mental health clinic, a small, well-equipped community hospital, and generalized social work services to deal with the emergencies which will arise. A community is not a real community until people have been born there, married there, and buried there. Provision for birth, marriage, illness, and death—*within the community*—is essential.

These communities must be open to the world to prevent the isolation, fragmentation, and specialization that will otherwise result. This means easy transportation, especially by air, as the ties of such men are wide and the spread of their special interests includes the whole country. But it should not only be easy to get away, it should also be easy for others to come there, and occasions for their coming should be planned. This requires the provision of comfortable and moderately expensive motels and guest houses, where all sorts of guests—temporary consultants, interns, foreign visitors, and so on—can be put up. A conference center with the accommodations for at least one hundred visitors is also recommended; this will bring groups to the community and favor the involvement of the technical community in nationwide activities.

There are other ways in which the diversification of the community at a high level can be attained: the location of colleges, special departments of universities, special research institutes that complement the principal technical interests represented. Recent developments in areas of California, where new electronic industries, special research institutes, and new branches of the University of California are combined, provide a good model here.

Further diversification can be attained if provision can be made for weekend and vacation facilities for various types of specialists in the arts and sciences who will be attracted by the caliber of the services and the opportunities to associate with a lively intellectual community. The biological laboratory at Woods Hole, Massachusetts, has represented such an attraction. Lawyers, high-level civil servants, journalists, physicians, residents in nearby urban centers, would welcome such a spot. These facilities should be of varying economic levels, suitable for graduate students finishing their theses, and families with many children and a couple of pets who arrive in a battered station wagon, as well as more established and wealthier people.

Communications within the community are vitally important so that everyone will know of the arrival of interesting visitors, the visits of people in the community to other communities, lectures, film showings, special school activities like the National Science Talent Search and Science Fairs, special broadcasts and telecasts. Freedom to move from institution to institution for special lectures or demonstrations is one of the ways in which such a community is welded together. The special technical community can become a lively, self-activated center for radiating intellectual and scientific interest by means of a small daily bulletin, local radio stations, and possibly closed television circuits with provision for diffusion throughout the community and to school auditoriums and places of assembly in other nearby centers.

Every imaginative effort put into planning such communities, and especially assuring the allocation of enough space for all of these activities, will benefit the wider interests of the state by raising the level of education, increasing the supply of future scientists, and assuring the type of community that is valuable for the ongoing economic life of the state.

In recent considerations of the way in which cultural evolution takes place and the possibility of man's taking a more active part in directing the course of his own intellectual evolution, it has been found useful to look for the occurrence of clusters of individuals who stimulate and complement each other's intellectual life. The surest way of developing such groups is to have clusters of institutions that will attract research-minded individuals of many different kinds and give them an environment that provides for their informal and voluntary interaction.

I have discussed here a specific model for one kind of development. Comparable models could be developed for small cities with different emphases—heavy industry centers, trade centers, educational centers, sports centers, and so on. Each type of city would have its special requirements for accessibility, design, and types of necessary diversification. One would be more appropriate than another, as a point of emphasis for small cities in different parts of a country, at different distances from the center of the country, from the capital city or metropolis and from other smaller or larger cities.

TYPES OF SUCCESSFUL AND UNSUCCESSFUL SMALL CITIES[2]

We may next look at contrasting types of cities, "good" cities and "bad" cities, which have developed within the same national economic and political framework. By concentrating on successful and unsuccessful histories within the same national potential, it is possible to highlight some of the factors which have made some small cities good and others bad, and use this analysis to direct the future growth and development of existing small cities.

First, let me consider a hypothetical small city in the middlewestern part of the United States, one with a population of over 150,000. What will be said about it is based on conditions generally found in small cities in the United States but is not a description of any particular one. I will call this composite portrait Center City. It has been adding new, light industries for some time. Its local Lions Club has visitors dropping in frequently who bring news of what clubs in other cities are doing and what speakers they have had at their meetings. These guests keep the members of the business and professional community on their toes. It has two newspapers, a morning and an evening paper, expressing different political views. Although they use a great deal of syndicated material that is distributed nationally, each newspaper carries its own editorials, and each has an editor personally known to the townspeople, who can complain directly to him if they do not like his paper's policy. Local issues are aired in the newspapers, and it is very difficult for some activity not in the public interest to go on for very long without an exposure.

Children of all races go to school together; there have been Negro teachers in the schools for twenty-five years; the basketball teams, of which the city has two first-class ones, have players drawn from different races. The salaries of the teachers are high, the standard of the high schools good, and every year high school graduates go away to college. They go not only to the state university and to the many nearby small private colleges supported by different religious organizations, but they also pass national college entrance examinations (and win scholarships for which there is national competition) to famous colleges and universities outside of the state.

The people of the city have seen to it that there is a big gymnasium for basketball games, school dances, science exhibits, educational exhibits, and teachers' institutes. Other meeting places—small halls in primary schools and junior high schools, and parish houses connected with the different churches—are plentiful enough so that there is room for all kinds of organizations to meet. There are three good hotels, which serve the luncheon clubs, Lions, Kiwanis, Rotary, the Chamber of Commerce, the Business and Professional Women's Club, and several smaller luncheon clubs.

Most of the industries are unionized; strikes hit the town only when they are part of a nation-wide strike, and there has never been a labor riot. In fact, there has never been a riot of any kind.

The center of the city is something the people are proud of. There is a wide open square with a fountain where children play in summer, a memorial to the men who died in the First World War. Around the square are the court house, one of the large old churches, a concert hall and theater. The city has its own orchestra and little theater repertory group, and it sponsors a series of concerts given by singers and musicians who are nationally and internationally known. A new shopping center has replaced some of the older stores on one side of the square, but without wrecking the design of the older buildings.

Traffic and parking are not too difficult. The city was one of the first to put in traffic lights; the Parent-Teacher Association has organized a corps of women volunteers to stand at the street corners where small children cross to go to school; the city put in parking meters as soon as these were for sale, and so never built up a set of bad parking habits. When the police say that they will pick up and haul away cars parked illegally, this is not just a threat: The cars are picked up and hauled away. Campaigns conducted jointly by the city police and a local chapter of the National Public Safety Association have cured pedestrians of crossing streets between crosswalks, and the City Improvement Society—it used to be called the Village Improvement Society—has put large waste-paper baskets for trash at every street corner, and these are used.

The library is almost a hundred years old, and a society called the Friends of the Public Library keeps up the appropriation for it from local taxes by appearing at City Hall for budget hearings. This group raises a considerable fund, each year, to buy new books, to pay for an extra librarian to work with the children, and to stock the steadily growing supply of tapes and recordings. A new library building, the fourth since the library was founded, is now being planned.

This city always goes over the top in every kind of fund-raising campaign. In the annual Community Chest drive the whole city is divided into sections—residential units and business units—and every citizen is included. An enormous number of local people are on the rolls of a national association for the prevention of tuberculosis and receive, each year, a packet of Christmas seals, for which each person pays a dollar. These seals are both for fund raising and to remind the public of the importance of the work of the association, and all the mail for several weeks before Christmas is decorated with them. There is a small Community Chest, a coordinating committee representing most of the local social agencies. Donations made to the Chest are distributed among the member agencies, so that people do not have to give to each one separately.

The local public agencies, which administer aid to families and dependent children, care for the needy old and blind, and provide health services to the community, have good relations with their state and federal counterparts. The representatives of these state and national agencies—professional, specially trained social workers, educators, public health workers—enjoy coming to this thriving little city and talking with the people in the local offices and giving talks to the service clubs and other organizations interested in the programs for human betterment they are there to foster. These include such concerns as mental health, parent education, air pollution, the education of handicapped and culturally disadvantaged children, more jobs for the unemployed, and the war on poverty. Center City responds warmly to the specialists who come into the community to discuss these concerns.

The schools have been alert to all the new possibilities in special educational programs. There are special classes for mentally retarded children, special teachers for house-bound children—youngsters who are recovering from operations and injuries or are suffering from chronic diseases—and special programs for the blind and hard of hearing. Deaf children are identified early and sent for their education to a nearby residential institution. There is a good foster home program, with more foster parents ready to take children from the public and private children's agencies than there are children to be placed. Unmarried mothers are given sympathetic care and their babies are sent to another city for adoption. There is a good juvenile court, the names of juvenile offenders are never published in the newspapers, and most children brought into juvenile court are placed on probation.

The local branch of the American Association of University Women has established and financed a mental health clinic for emotionally disturbed children. In this association, the high school teachers play a leading role. Most of them have been in Center City for many years and taught generations of Center City children. The city has three private schools, one coeducational, one for boys, and one for girls, all of which began under religious auspices and are now nonsectarian, and a junior community college, which will soon become a four-year college. Its faculty takes an active part in community affairs. There is a small art museum, liberally supported by some of the older families in the community, and an organized society of supporters who work for it, arranging, for instance, for Saturday classes in painting and for public lectures.

People who live in Center City agree that this is a good city to live in. Many young people born and educated there do not want to move away and, in order to stay, will take local jobs at lower salaries than they could earn elsewhere. Young executives who are placed there in branch offices of large corporations often refuse to take the next step up in their organizations if this means leaving Center City. High school teachers qualified for college teaching stay on here as high school teachers rather than go away to university positions.

People are so proud of what their city has done and is doing that it is very hard for them to see that more needs to be done—which is, in fact, a great deal. Interest in international affairs has never been very intense. There is a United Nations Association, but it does very little except plan school programs for United Nations Day. There is a Center City Mental Health Association, which provides a way for interested professional people, like social workers and community-minded doctors, to meet with interested lay people, but no one in this local group seems very much concerned about the State Mental Health Association, and none of them are members of the World Federation for Mental Health.

The recent agitations for civil rights for Negroes have practically by-passed this small city. It is true that it is still hard for middle-class Negroes here to get the same kind of credit conditions that are available for white people or to buy homes in new middle-class housing developments, but relationships between the small Negro professional group, the Negro community as a whole, and the rest of the town have always been so good that it is very difficult to get people to bestir themselves about the problems that are not yet solved. Years ago, there was some excitement over having Negro teachers in the public schools; two were employed and the excitement subsided. There have not been any more Negro teachers added, not because there is the slightest objection to having them, but because they are hard to recruit and those who might be out looking for them are making no effort. The racial imbalance in the teaching corps is evident; school officials have become so *tolerant* that they see no reason for making it an issue.

There is a very small Jewish community, and the rabbi is invited once a year to give the invocation at a meeting of each important community organization. After the inauguration of President Kennedy, when prayers were offered by Roman Catholic, Jewish, Protestant, and Eastern Orthodox clergy, several Center Citizens asked if there was an Eastern Orthodox church in town and found that there was not. A few Spanish-speaking Puerto Ricans have moved in lately, and a community group got together some money to send a teacher to Puerto Rico to learn something about the Puerto Rican children's background.

Only in time of war or some other great national crisis does a "good" community like this wake up and try to become a better community, to compare itself not only with all the neighboring cities, where it already excels, but with national averages for different kinds of achievement. And it will only be thoroughly awakened from its accustomed round of excellent activities if national pressure, exerted through radio, television, and the press is very strong.

In the early 1960's, the national concern about children who drop out of school before graduation pierced the complacency of Center City. The Parent-Teacher Associations, the American Association of University Women, three service clubs—Kiwanis, Lions, and Rotary—the local chapter of the Association for Childhood Education International, and of the National Education Association, the Mental Health Society, the Society for the Support of the Arts, the City Improvement Society, and representatives of the coordinating council of the Community Chest, all worked on the dropout problem with the city superintendent of schools and his staff of principals.

This meant getting all the national literature: finding out what their own state was doing and, for each organization, what its national office was doing; getting a list of good speakers who could deal with different aspects of the problem; finding out what programs were already going on; deciding whether to try some plan that had been tried or make an innovation.

Someone recalled an innovation made during World War II, when the brighter, older children in the high schools had been organized to help relieve the teacher shortage by tutoring younger cihldren who were falling behind in their studies. It was a plan that had been dropped after the war because teachers, poorly paid and overworked, had developed an overprofessional attitude toward teaching and did not want volunteers to interfere with their attempts to raise standards and salaries. Now that it was clear that an important new national program would require a great deal of volunteer help to get started, the groups working on the dropout problem decided to use students again. When New York City in 1967 inaugurated a plan to pay older pupils to teach younger children who were falling behind, this resulted in national publicity and reinforced the local effort.

Center City, then, has the virtues of the best small American cities. People are proud to live there. They boast that every child gets a chance to go to some sort of summer camp, that their high school graduates have the best records in the state.

But the enthusiasm of its citizens is not the only reason for the prosperity of this city. It is just the right distance from two very large cities in a part of a state where industry has flourished. The plants located here are in expanding industries. The first labor union to enter the town was a particularly enlightened one. None of the local industries were deeply involved in army contracts, so cutbacks and expansions in armaments have not affected them badly. Nor have they yet felt the impact of automation; several of the major industries were partly automated earlier.

The owners of the two newspapers are independently wealthy and, so far, have not had to sell out to syndicates. There have been three competent school superintendents in a row. There is a good, small airport because several of the sons of prominent families like to fly and their demands for an airport were supported by townspeople who thought the city ought to have one. There is an excellent supply of fresh water; the streets are well laid out, with residential areas nicely dispersed. Industry is electrified, and the air is not yet polluted, as it is in so many other places, by the fumes from cars and factories. And, finally, the city has never had to deal with an influx of people from terribly disadvantaged areas, people badly schooled, in poor health, bearing the marks of generations of neglect.

For some of these things, Center City residents can take credit because, in spite of all these advantages, the town could be in bad shape if it had not had lively leadership, ready contributions of time and money, esprit de corps, the loyalty of its hard-working citizens. But these same citizens tend to take responsibility for everything good, and to blame everything that goes wrong on "circumstances beyond our control."

There are unmarried mothers here, juvenile delinquents, frauds and robberies, corrupt politicians, small but unmistakable slums, deprived children, broken homes, sex crimes, miserable old people, high school dropouts, mothers who receive no prenatal care, discriminations against minorities, children whose expectations are dimmed and futures ruined because they feel that they come from a background which never has been and never will be accepted.

But when the people of our lively, intelligent, favored little city have to face these things, they disclaim all responsibility for them. Failures in school? The parents have probably moved too often. Discrimination? Not among us; it must be those new people. Vandalism? That comes from the glorification of violence and crime on television and in the movies. *Our* people don't behave like that. Why, even when we do lock our doors, everybody knows where the keys are kept.

It is not likely that Center City will produce many ardent reformers, even from among its most disadvantaged and rebellious citizens. Advantaged or disadvantaged, young people growing up here feel that it is a good place to live, that if they fail as individuals, this must be their own fault since theirs is such a good city. It is a city which may not even produce many young people who want to join the Peace

Corps or Vista; the very complete and adequate social services of their own town have not awakened in them any sharp awareness of other people's needs. The Center City post office sends out a flood of parcels at Christmas time for persons all over the world, but many of those who mail them gladly criticize the federal government harshly for "giving away things," meaning by that its programs of social welfare and foreign aid. A good many people who want every dollar of state and federal money they can get for local activities they are interested in, will greet the slightest suggestion from their state capital or from Washington with suspicion, crying "the federal government is trying to take over the country."

So it is important to recognize that an American community that runs the way an American community is supposed to run can do it almost too successfully—so successfully that its citizens become too complacent. Though it is a city that keeps many of its promising people, it is not a city to which successful people from larger cities would like to move. There is something too provincial about its complacency. This complacency can be challenged if the community is compared unfavorably with some other city of roughly the same size. The accomplishments of great cities have little meaning for Center City, and the achievements of smaller cities stir no interest there. As long as other places of the same size are not doing better, Center City will rest on its laurels, unless something tremendous shakes it out of its self-satisfaction. In such communities, striving has become maintenance, and aspiration has turned into justifiable but self-defeating pride.

But there are other cities of the same size in the United States that present an almost exactly opposite picture. Let us take another composite example and call it Border City. Border City lies not inside a prosperous state but on the border between two states, one much more prosperous than the other. Part of the city is in one state, part in the other. Any attempt to unify services which need state or national help runs immediately into problems of jurisdiction. Every time someone moves from one part of the city to the other, he goes into another world. He must get a new license for his car, pay a different state income tax, comply with a different set of marriage laws, meet different requirements for various kinds of insurance.

Education on any public issue is difficult in Border City, again because there are two states involved. Whereas in Center City, state, county, and city work so closely together that most citizens do not know where one begins and the other ends, here there is constant dispute over which authority has the right to do what. A sick man may be driven to a hospital, only to find that he cannot be cared for at this institution because he lives on the other side of the state line. If there is a question of public relief or compensation in his case, and the hospital does take him in as an emergency, it may take months of paper work to decide who pays for him. When responsible citizens in the upper, more prosperous part of the city try to clean up conditions they feel are producing a bad environment for their young people, they are continually foiled by the other side, where there is open gambling, much teen-age drinking, open sale of drugs, and a corrupt police force that interferes with their attempts to enforce the law. Migrant workers, homeless and destitute, pour into the lower city first, then cross over easily and become part of a faceless welfare load on the other side.

Border City started as a mill town, but the owners of the mills soon moved away to a nearby large city. Hired managers, who were often unfriendly to the town, took their places. One industry after another has come in to take advantage of the cheap labor available here, using first immigrants then rural migrants who have followed their friends and relatives into town.

As there were no professional people here, originally, the city has no core of old professional families; no sons or nephews come back to take over the medical practices of fathers or uncles; no young men to go into family law firms. The professional people who do come here do not usually come by choice and do not stay if there is anywhere else for them to go. The schools, long a political football, have a superintendent who seems utterly uninterested in standards of any kind.

A long series of strikes left the union leaders and small business and professional men at loggerheads, with no body of stable, responsible old inhabitants to mediate the differences. Housing is run down, and the few housing developments built during World War II are dilapidated and occupied by families on relief rolls. In most American cities, the local political organization is built with the votes of individual citizens. In Border City, the politicians work for blocks of votes, to be delivered through the leaders of the four principal ethnic groups: a southern European group, an old United Kingdom group, an eastern European group, and a sizable group of Negroes, recent immigrants from the South. There is no attempt to conceal political patronage.

There is an old public library, started years ago by a small, eager college club composed of half a dozen school teachers and two ministers' wives. This little group managed to take their plea for a library for Border City all the way to Andrew Carnegie, who built or helped to build so many libraries in American communities. But there is not enough money, now, to give good library service. The librarians are poorly paid; the city council is not interested in appropriating funds. Because of a shortage of staff, the children's room can only be open part of the time.

Instead of the full complement of organizations which kept Center City humming, there are very few in Border City: some Lodges, a dispirited Rotary Club, a few groups connected with churches. The church leadership is weak; assignment to a pastoral charge here is considered a hardship, not a challenge. Most of the school teachers come from homes where there were no books; to them, education is a new, almost frightening experience. There is no bookstore in town, no museum, no large hall where lectures could be heard, no lecture series bringing distinguished, nationally known speakers, no little theater group, no concerts. The two newspapers are both owned and operated by a national newspaper syndicate; one is probably going out of business soon because there is not enough advertising to keep it going. There is no institution of higher learning of any kind, no modern industrial plant to bring a corps of lively young engineers, not even a normal school that might become a teachers' college.

48

The center of the city is grubby and run down, but it does not face the kind of deterioration that larger, fairer cities do because it never had either style or beauty, and there were no old families there to move away and leave houses that became rat-infested slums. The city is not growing and unemployment is rising as industries adopt new labor-saving devices. Large numbers of young people drop out of school to look for work as soon as the law permits them to do so. The fact that the age of compulsory education is two years higher in one part of the city than in the other, because the two parts are in different states, adds to the tension.

The established churches are poorly attended and find it hard to get committees responsible enough to handle their affairs. There are many so-called "store-front churches"—store buildings used by small sects for services because they are too poor to have their own houses of worship or to pay for full-time pastors.

The schools are miserable. The children clique together, perpetuating religious and ethnic hostilities. Those who do finish high school with some ambition for more education will go on to the nearest—the poorer—state teachers' college. Very few will even try for the state university. In the Border City schools there are no teachers to nurture their ambitions, no young people's organizations to stir up their hopes. Returned missionaries, who travel from community to community telling congregations about their educational work with children in other countries, pass Border City by. It is notorious for meager contributions, for never meeting its quota in national drives for causes like the Red Cross.

Here, there is very little hope that sparks will fly or that some young and vivid reformer will raise his head. There is every reason to believe that each of these cities has as many innately intelligent children as the other. But in one of these cities every community agency and institution works for the children, protecting their health as infants, seeing to it that they have good preschool care, giving them stimulating grade school experiences, providing wholesome opportunities for their leisure. In the other city, medical care is poor; there are no nursery schools, kindergartens, or Head Start classes. Aid to dependent children is given without supervision; the primary schools are crowded, poorly equipped, and the children are badly taught; in the high schools, the chief interest is the band.

Both are American cities. Both have access to the same state and federal matching funds for improving, expanding, and introducing all sorts of programs; both have, theoretically, the same access to such other sources of funds and consultation services as national foundations and state and national offices of voluntary organizations. In one place historical conditions combined positively to produce a city in which the sense of community has flourished. In the other, historical conditions have had an opposite outcome. The same national agencies, the same state agencies, the same foundations, the same national organizations, and the same human potentialities were there for each to draw upon. The children have read the same history books in school, and memorized the same sentiments. The same national television shows have been reflected on screens in both cities. But in one, the community was able to take advantage of all this; in the other it was not.

Center City and Border City are not to be found on any American road map, or in any railway guide, because they do not actually exist. They are composite pictures representing the extremes of American community life. Because each community in the United States is free, within reasonable limits, to become the kind of hamlet, village, town, or city that its people want it to be, community life in any one of them can be raised to a very high standard or sink to a very low one.

At present, neither Center City nor Border City seems likely to generate leadership for change: one is too complacent, the other too miserable. The impact of a powerful national program might help to start community action in either place. Cities like Center City do sometimes come out of their comfortable shells, and things sometimes do get going in places like Border City. A small city may receive a bequest which gives it a college, for example, or a museum, or enable it to employ a magnificent superintendent of schools or a forward-looking city manager. A new kind of industrial plant may come in and its management, used to cities with some life in them, goes to work. But Center City has a long, long start in the kind of institutions that lead to responsible change.

It is right here that the state and national program can have an impact. Spurred by knowledge of what is going on in the state, the nation, or the world, they can take the lead in starting a college or a museum, or in bringing in a new kind of city management and a new kind of urban planning.

PLANNED NEW SMALL CITIES

The possibilities inherent in old small cities may be contrasted with the planned new small cities which are now on the drawing boards or partly completed. Behind the plans for these new ready-made communities lies more or less the same assumption: if the physical environment is right, life for the people in it will be good. Such cities, the promoters say, offer a new opportunity to meet the challenge of growth. They stress the economic advantage to the community, the county, and the state through the planned use of space and the careful integration of the new town into the economic structure of the region.

In such designs, there are a number of small towns or villages within the city, with different types of residential neighborhoods in each one. Each will have its own schools, parks, churches, shops, and other appropriate businesses and services. The industries will be, for the most part, very tidy ones—research and development laboratories, offices, and plants for light manufacturing. Each part of the city will be linked to every other part by small buses, traveling on roads especially built for them. The idea is to make the development so completely self-sustaining and so well-arranged that everything a family needs will be within walking distance of its home or on a local bus line. It is expected that many people will give up cars altogether, or use them only for trips out of the community. Actually, the local buses will connect with the regular intercity, interstate buses on the superhighways that pass by the town. In fifteen years, one such city, planned for families with an average income of about $9,000 a year, could provide homes for about 29,000 families, approximately 110,000 people. Other new cities are planned to have homes at different prices for families in a wide range of income brackets.

DYNAMIC CITY-INDUSTRY PARTNERSHIP

To Americans who believe that the best communities are created and continually reconstructed by the people who live in them, these new, planned communities are somewhat disconcerting. It is encouraging to turn, at this point, to look at a town that enjoys a remarkably rich and delightful community life because it has a dynamic, working partnership with a thriving industry.

This town is Corning, New York. It sits on the banks of the Chemung River, in one of the prettiest parts of the state. Settled in 1789, it now has a population of about 17,000. Electrical and railroad supplies, tools, saws, and furnaces are manufactured here, but the chief source of pride is the world-famous Corning Glass Works. This is the firm that in 1934 made the 200-inch lens for the telescope of Mount Palomar Observatory in California and produces, among other things, the exquisite and costly Steuben glass.

This company is a small-town family business founded in 1851. It moved to Corning in 1868 and has grown to giant size. It now has, together with its subsidiaries, 45 factories in 15 states. An article about the Glass Works in *Fortune Magazine* for August 1964 describes it as "the company that never left town." Its present chairman and chief executive officer, Amory Houghton, Jr., a young man now only 42 years of age, is the fifth generation of his family to run the factory, having come up through the company with experience in nearly every branch of the organization.

52

The Glass Works and the town are in real partnership and are equally appreciative of each other. Whatever is done in the community, they do together. From the beginning, it has been company policy to encourage local independence and citizen initiative by giving in such a way that the gifts help the town do its own growing.

Some of the results of this joint venture are widely recognized. There is a good school system, as progressive as any in New York State, which has some of the best teachers in the country. There is a non-profit hospital and a library that serves as a library center for 100,000 people in that part of the state. There are excellent recreation facilities: choral and square dance groups, a glider site, swimming pools, a ski run, and an ice-skating rink, picnic areas and a toboggan slide. All of these are set up for families to use and enjoy.

Contributions from the glass company are more or less concentrated in two areas: community improvement and education. The most spectacular thing it has created cuts across both areas of its interest, and is a service to the whole country, not just the town of Corning. This the Corning Glass Center, a modern Crystal Palace, which commemorated the one hundredth anniversary of the firm and, by coincidence, the centennial of the original Crystal Palace in London, England.

The building includes a large auditorium for community and company use; a lobby where the first casting of the 200-inch lens has been placed upright against the wall facing the entrance, a wall covered with soft draperies of the blue of the midnight sky; one of the most complete glass museums in the world; a Hall of Science and Industry, where the nature and use of glass are shown with the aid of lectures and modern visual aids: exhibits, demonstrations, dioramas, films, recordings, and slides; the Steuben factory, where the visitor can actually see fine handblown crystal being formed and engraved; two auditoriums seating, respectively, 100 and 1,100 people. This is not only a center for the display of one of man's great discoveries, the process of glassmaking, it is also a center for the people who work with this material.

The Corning Glass Center is a source of wonder and delight to the three-quarter million people who visit it each year and these visitors have helped the town in many ways. The local stores have greatly increased their businesses since the Center was opened, and the hotels, restaurants, and motels—many of them new—have brought in large amounts of additional revenue. The company has benefited, too, because everything done to make Corning and the neighboring villages attractive to employees and their families makes it easier for the firm to find and keep the kinds of people who meet their very high employment standards.

Contributions made by the company in the field of education are carefully considered for their "seeding" value. High-level national conferences are held in the Glass Center from time to time, meetings which have an influence on national policies in many fields of science and the humanities. These, too, become the concern of the entire community. When the first one was held, to celebrate the opening of the museum, everybody in town worked to get it ready on time, and when the guests came from abroad, a role in the plans for their reception was found for every group in town, including the local fire company, which took over the task of shining all the foreign visitors' shoes.

Opportunities for the in-service training of teachers in the schools are varied and good. A community college was established in 1956 as a unit of the State University of New York. This has had a measurable effect on Corning and the adjacent communities. Since it opened, the library circulation has doubled, book sales in the town have increased, a cooperative nurses' training program has been developed in the Corning hospital, and the college has also set up industrial courses to train for local business and industry.

Seven small colleges in the area are being helped to strengthen their programs through a cooperative venture known as the College Center of the Finger Lakes, the headquarters of which are at Houghton House in Corning. The possibility of establishing a national headquarters here for cooperation in education is being considered. Contributions made by employees of the Glass Works to educational institutions are matched by the company. In 1967, these employee gifts amounted to $66,000.

Grants are made to enable teachers to study in the summer time, not only in Corning but in other company plant towns. About one hundred teachers are chosen from all communities where the company has plants, and the maximum grant is $600. An annual College Day is held in Corning for students, parents, and guidance counselors, to acquaint people with what different American colleges and universities have to offer. Grants are made to the Corning School District for educational television programs in the schools, and small capital awards are frequently made to projects that will become self-supporting, such as a program for gifted students, the Corning Philharmonic Society, and an exhibit arranged by the National Sculpture Society. In 1951, the Corning Glass Works established the Corning Glass Works Foundation to plan and coordinate its wide spectrum of activities in cooperation with the people of Corning and other communities with which it works. In 1964, the Foundation set aside funds for a conference on Africa, in cooperation with the Foundation for Youth and Student Affairs. The meeting was held in Corning and combined discussions with a study of the Corning area, which includes several colleges and universities, and provided an opportunity to become acquainted with the workings of local government in a special situation—an industrial community within an agricultural economy.

In a country with more than 200 million people and more than 18,000 population centers, of all shapes and sizes, there are sure to be communities as complacent as Center City, as depressed as Border City, as efficient as the new planned cities, and as fortunate as Corning, in some degree. As each one is able to take what it has and make what it wants, within the framework of the American value system, the possibilities for growth are very great.

It is in situations like these, as some impetus makes change possible, that institutions like the Lions Clubs can have a real impact. They can take the lead in attracting a new and lively industry, in exploiting some natural advantage, in getting a college started, or a new shopping center with a community center. They can, if their attention is focused on their role in urbanization, tip the balance, away from provincial complacency in the good cities and towards growth and development in the bad cities.

THE NEED FOR QUALITY NOT QUANTITY, DEVELOPMENT RATHER THAN GROWTH

But there is one further problem that must be faced if the small city is to play an important role in the future. It must not only hold some of its own best young people, but it must also attract gifted and enterprising people from larger cities, people who will value the advantages that can be found in a developing small city. It must not only maintain the sound institutions that it has, but it must provide for development within them: a small library must become a bigger library; a radio station must be replaced by a TV station; the old opera house or concert hall must become a modern theater; the normal school a four-year college, the college a university, the university add a medical school. As old industries decay, new growing industries must replace them. An old hotel must not be allowed to close its doors until new motels with adequate banquet facilities have been built.

If a city is to have the kind of character that will keep some of its best people and attract others, there must be a sense that it is developing. In the past those cities that have achieved this have done so primarily by a growth in numbers. It is true that some cities have gone steadily downhill without an appreciable loss in numbers, simply by the substitutions of less-able people for the more-able people who moved away. But the cities which have been able to generate a large amount of enthusiasm have been cities which were growing steadily in numbers. But growth in numbers is not what we must aim at today. If the small city is to make its most distinctive contribution, it must remain a *small* city, a city where distances are not too great, a city where all the interested citizenry take part in the same activities, a city big enough for surprises and new encounters but small enough so that all the citizenry feel a connection with the political, economic, artistic and intellectual life of the city.[3] So it is necessary to replace a growth in the number of institutions by an improvement in their quality, higher standards, increased national and international participation, increased ways of attracting outside activities, temporarily or, occasionally, permanently into the community without increasing its size. Those institutions, such as service clubs, who are the promoters of civic well-being will need new forms of reckoning up their progress, in upgrading, in ever higher replacement of the old by the new. Small cities as small cities have a bright future and an important contribution to make. Small cities that become overgrown and unmanageable, air polluted and overstrained, sprawling among uncoordinated suburban developments only add to the problems of today's world. Their essential and challenging problem is how to develop without growing bigger.

NOTES

1. Margaret Mead, "Building Communities for the Builders of Tomorrow," in Sterling Forest *Symposium on "Research and the Community." May 1, 1961 under the Auspices of the New York State Advisory Council for the Advancement of Industrial Research and Development* (Albany: Department of Commerce, State of New York, 1962), pp. 47-54.

2. Margaret Mead and Muriel Brown, *The Wagon and the Star: A Study of American Community Initiative* (St. Paul, Minn.: Curriculum Resources, 1966; reprinted Chicago: Rand McNally, 1967).

3. Margaret Mead, "Values for Urban Living," *Annals of the American Academy of Political and Social Science,* CXIV (November 1957), pp. 10-14; "1. The City as a Point of Confrontation. 2. Megalopolis: Is It Inevitable?" *Transactions of the Bartlett Society,* II (1965), pp. 9-22, 23-41.

3

Masatoshi Matsushita

Tokyo in 2000 A.D.

If I live in the year 2000 A.D., I shall be 99 years old, an old man indeed. Still, I shall be seventy years younger than Sirai Baba Mislimoff, the oldest man in the world of our times, for it is stated that he was born in 1805. I hope that I shall live in the year 2000, provided that 2000 is better than 1968. The world, however, will not become better or worse by natural course. Man can make it better if he tries and if he possesses faith and courage and wisdom. Admitting all negative elements, I think that the balance is favorable for optimism. I think that among us the requisite virtues exist. I think that in 2000 A.D. the world will become a world much better than the one we now know, and I am glad that I am called upon in these interim years to exercise such faith, such courage and such wisdom as I may possess to make this not an idle hope, but reality. That which I see within the three decades ahead of us is change—change more vast than anything which we have yet experienced—and I see difficulties proportionate to that change which we must surmount. It is because of that change and because of those certain difficulties that we dare to look to the future if faith, courage, and wisdom are our aides. Holding to the idea of the fundamental equality of Man and Man's capacity to adapt himself to any new environment, we possess, by my definition, faith. Faith is essential to face change. By possessing the will to overcome those certain difficulties which we shall encounter, we possess, by my definition, courage. Courage is essential to surmount difficulties. And, by my definition, having farsighted vision, a proper caution, and the sense of good order, we have wisdom. Wisdom is imperative for Man to be able to confront change and to win over his trials. Wisdom must be our guide. Using Paulean rhetoric, "though Man has Faith and Courage and has not Wisdom, they profit him nothing." Such is my creed and such is my premise for optimism.

I shall proceed now to the exercise of my thesis, fearless of criticism, opposition, obstacles, or even the determined enemy who would destroy Man's will to be free, and I shall take joy in my task. My task is the call of wisdom to consider soberly the multiplying problems of Tokyo as she approaches the year 2000 and to endeavor to find what shall be required for their solutions. My thesis is that the problems which Japan faces concerning Tokyo, Japan cannot solve alone. Tokyo is an international problem.

Let us begin by recognizing facts and situations as they exist. Then, by means of the best evidence available to us, let us examine the picture of Tokyo as it is most likely to be in a score and ten years hence. This done, I shall offer a proposal, one that I could not offer had I not the conviction that Man does possess those virtues, which I quite firmly believe are requisite for his survival.

The world in 1968 is in a most confused stage of its development. This stage cannot last long. Western Europe, the United States, and other so-called developed countries enjoy political and economic stability, and their peoples are maintaining relatively high standards of living. On the other hand, in vast areas of Asia, Africa and South America, the peoples are living next to starvation. We will find solutions, or we will find destruction. I say we will find solutions.

Japan is the only developed country among nonwhite countries. Recognition of this fact by the world has been the cause of pride for its people. This fact, however, is the cause for Japan's having to assume heavy responsibility within a time now rapidly approaching, and this fact is the cause even of anxiety. This argument is not solely a moral or theoretical one. The simple fact is that Japan is surrounded by undeveloped countries, and in consideration of her close historical and economic ties with these countries, it is demanded of Japan that she take some kind of leadership in making these undeveloped nations truly developing ones. This, of course, Japan cannot do alone. The whole-hearted cooperation of other Asiatic countries is necessary. From other developed countries aid and assistance of various kinds are needed, and they are providing such help directly or indirectly through international organizations, because they are fully cognizant of the significance and implications of the problem. The point which I should like to emphasize is that Japan is particularly affected by the confused conditions of Asia. We must take up this problem and consider it not the problem of other countries but our own. To say it directly, the problems of Asia are our own domestic problems. Unless we face this reality now and adopt courageous policies, the future of Japan will be very dark.

Our first imperative is to fully understand the problems in Asia. The most serious problem in Asia is poverty. The root of the problem lies in overpopulation, by which we mean the imbalance between the increase of population and the production of food. In a sense, over-population is a world problem, not just Asia's.

In 1945 the total population of the world was 2.3 billion. In 1965 the population of the world had increased to 3.3 billion. This shows the average increase of 50 million people per year. If we take the total population of three billion for 1960 as our basis, the average increase per year to 1965 is 60 million. This means that a country the size of England, France, or Italy is made every year. This tendency toward increase is not likely to stop. According to an estimate made in 1963 by the United Nations, the total population of the world will reach 4.487-billion in 1980, 5.7 billion in 1990, and 7.41 billion in 2000, based on the rate of a 3 per cent increase for the last ten years.

This population explosion is not followed by a corresponding ratio of food production. Of the present total world population of 3.3 billion approximately one billion belong to the advanced countries of the world like the United States, Western Europe, Canada, and Japan. The remaining 2.3 billion belong to the less-developed areas like Asia, Africa, and South America. In these areas, the population, the two-thirds of the world's people, are either undernourished or mal-nourished. From the same FAO report we take the statement that over 2 billion inhabitants of these areas have an intake of food of less than 2,300 calories per day per capita.

Although numerous other facts and figures could be brought forth and listed here, the foregoing are sufficient to clearly state that over-population is a world problem, and, therefore, should be solved ulti-mately by a world organization, such as the United Nations.

What I want to stress, however, is that the problems of poverty, population and food are particularly urgent and pressing in Asia. The following figures will prove my point.

WORLD POPULATION, BY EIGHT MAJOR AREAS, ESTIMATED ACCORDING TO THE ASSUMPTION OF "CONTINUED RECENT TRENDS," 1960-2000

Provisional Report on World Population Prospect Assumed by the United Nations in 1963

POPULATION (millions)

	1960	1970	1980	1990	2000
World total	2,990	3,626	4,487	5,704	7,410
More-developed areas	854	851	1,085	1,230	1,393
Europe	425	460	496	533	571
Soviet Union	214	253	295	345	402
Northern America	199	230	270	325	388
Oceania	15.7	18.4	22.0	26.7	32.5
Less-developed areas	2,136	2,665	3,402	4,474	6,017
East Asia	793	941	1,139	1,419	1,803
South Asia	858	1,092	1,418	1,898	2,598
Africa	273	348	458	620	860
Latin America	212	284	387	537	756
Northern areas	1,631	1,884	2,202	2,622	3,164
Southern areas	1,359	1,742	2,285	3,082	4,246

In 1960 the total population of Asia was 1.651 billion; the world population was 2.99 billion. In 2000 the total population in Asia will be 4.401 billion; the world population, 7.41 billion. In either case, the population of Asia is more than half of that of the world. Among the less-developed areas, Africa and South America have rich natural resources; Asia has far less, and the problem is more serious where natural resources are lacking.

The above brings Asia to the point of asking what it should do. I am not suggesting that we despair. I am suggesting, on the contrary, that we must remove this difficulty with the faith and courage and wisdom that we possess. Were things always easy, there would be no opportunity for us to cultivate these virtues, and we would degenerate unless we do. It is difficulties, indeed serious ones, that make Man full of faith, courageous, and wise. Therefore, far from being given to despair or from becoming resentful, we should be thankful for the serious problems we are facing.

I think that there are numerous ways to make things better in Asia and in the world. My good friend Professor Kaigo Noma, at the Third Freedom from Hunger Campaign Conference sponsored by FAO, made highly constructive proposals, including the immediate development of tropical zones. This and other such constructive proposals should be seriously considered and discussed, together with the question of birth control. The important point is that all proposals should be well balanced and correlated. No problem should be considered to exclude other problems. We need a system of cybernetics for proposals made, that men may go to work at once in studying them in an orderly and necessary way.

What I am leading toward is a suggestion for a partial solution of Asia's problem, a suggestion which should be correlated and integrated with other plans. I think that Tokyo can play an important role in solving the problems which we have been considering. It is already the largest metropolis in the world and it is still growing. As to this statement, skeptics may raise objection, saying that Tokyo is the largest metropolis only in the sense that Tokyo-to consists of 23 wards and three tama-gun, which is but a product of administrative convenience, and in this it is larger than any other competing metropolis, such as New York or London. They will say that the real Tokyo is large, but it is not necessarily the largest metropolis in the world. This argument sounds plausible, but it has no scientific ground for being made. The truth of the matter is that Tokyo in reality is much larger than Tokyo-to. Let me cite the case.

In 1965 the total population of the 23 wards which comprise the center of Tokyo-to was 8.9 million, and the total population of Tokyo-to was 10.9 million. The area of these 23 wards, the core of the metropolis, is 15 km. The core of the metropolitan area of New York has a 7.8 million population and the core of London's only 3.2 million. Insofar as density is concerned, Tokyo's is thus the largest. This fact, of course, is not greatly important. The most important aspect of our argument concerns the number of persons working and deriving income in Tokyo, regardless of the locations of their dwellings. If we do this, we must extend Tokyo-to to a 50 km circle from its center, and this would include Kanagawa, Saitama, and Chiba. The combined population of this 50 km circle in 1965 was 21 million. This is the real Tokyo. If we compare the real Tokyo with the other competing metropolises, no skeptic could raise objection. The 50 km circle of New York has 13 million inhabitants; were we to extend the circle to 100 km, there would only be 16 million inhabitants. To do the same for Tokyo, there would be 27 million people found living within the orbit of that city. London is out of the race. Within a 50 km circle of London, there are only 10 million population. By all of this, it is therefore firmly established that Tokyo is the largest metropolis in the world in every respect.

As to Tokyo's population growth, the figures are impressive. The general belief is that Tokyo's recent population growth is slacking. This belief is but a partial truth. From 1950 to 1955 the annual growth of the city was 320,000 people; in 1955-1960 it was 870,000; in 1966-1965 it was 120,000. These figures refer to Tokyo-to. However, if we take into consideration the growth rate of the real Tokyo, that is to say, the 50 km. circle, the annual growth in 1950-1955 was 470,000; in 1955-1960, 490,000; in 1960-1965, 630,000. Therefore, with regard to the growth of Tokyo, it is enjoying the highest rate. How long will this tendency continue? According to estimates of the Research Institute of Population of the Welfare Department, the population of the 50 km circle around Tokyo will reach 30.5 million in 1980 and 38.4 million in 1995. These figures, however, seem to have been underestimated.

Other figures would indicate that a 40 million metropolitan population will be reached by 1970, an 80 million population by 1980, and a 110 million population by the year 2000. Even if this estimate is true, I do not think that Tokyo will absorb all these people. However, unless some positive measures are taken, 60 to 70 per cent of the estimated population will be absorbed by this metropolis, and this means 60 to 70 million persons by the year 2000. Is this physically possible? Yes, it is possible, provided that we take the necessary measures, such as the construction of vertical buildings, the reduction of unnecessary transportation, and so on.

Before proceeding further, I should like to consider the causes of this rapid growth. They are two. One is the technological revolution, common to all advanced countries. In this respect, Tokyo is in the same category as New York, London, Chicago, Paris, and Moscow. As technology advances, the population of Tokyo will naturally grow. The other cause, however, is peculiarly Japanese. Tokyo and other metropolises are rapidly absorbing agricultural population. That is why Tokyo is growing so fast. It also indicates that there is still an abundant agricultural population in Japan. To give this picture clearly, listing agriculture's rating first beside Japan's second and third largest industries, agriculture's profile looks like this: In 1955 agriculture's proportion of Japan's industry was 41.0 per cent compared with 35.5 per cent and 23.5 per cent of the second and third largest industries. In 1960 the proportions changed to 32.6 per cent, 38.2 per cent, and 29.2 per cent. According to estimates of the Economic Planning Board, it will be 23.5 per cent, 33.5 per cent, and 43 per cent after ten years; and after twenty years, 15.6 per cent, 40.8 per cent and 43.6 per cent. At the end of this century, the Board estimates that the nation's former first industry will be reduced to less than 7 per cent. It is an important factor that Japan, highly advanced and industrialized as any other Western country, still has more than a 30 per cent agricultural population. London is growing slowly, because England's agricultural population is already only 4 per cent. New York is growing more rapidly, because the agricultural population of the United States is now about 10 per

cent. Estimates are that Tokyo will continue to grow until the agricultural population of Japan is reduced to 7 per cent of the total population in the year 2000. Based upon the records and the experience of
the past, the estimates of this report, I would say, are largely correct.
However, this report neglects a very important factor, that is, that Japan
is an Asiatic country, surrounded by less-developed countries. What
does this mean?

Thus far, all our estimates have been compiled in a national sense:
Tokyo and Japan, London and England, New York and the United
States. The logic is valid in Europe and in the United States, for there is
little possibility that a large-scale migration of peoples will be made in
the future. The United States is a country of emigrants. There was a
large-scale migration of population to that country in the seventeenth,
eighteenth and nineteenth centuries, but since the beginning of the
twentieth century, migration has decreased. In Europe, there is little
possibility of there being a large-scale migration in the future. Therefore, there is a valid reason why countries like these have estimated the
rates of growth of their urban populations with reference to the proportion of their agricultural populations. And there is a valid reason
why Japan could make its estimates in the same way, for there has not
been a large-scale migration of population in Asia. But the question is,
can or should we assume that what was valid in the past will be valid
for the future and should be followed? I do not think so.

The time will come sooner or later when there will be a large-
scale Asiatic migration to Japan. If we do not predict this inevitability,
and if we do not willingly invite these peoples, they will come to us
against our will. It is in the course of nature that people of overpopulated, less-advanced countries seek to come to better land. It was
the case with the Germanic invasion of Rome in the second century. It
was the case of the Norman Conquest in the eleventh century. It was
the case of the various "barbarian" invasions of China. Most Asiatic
countries, except Japan, were either colonies or half colonies of other
nations, and Asiatic populations could not freely migrate. They had no

66

habit of migration. They still do not. That is why, dissatisfied with their miserable lives in agriculture, these peoples seek better lives in their own metropolises and find themselves still more miserable. The shifting from one bad place to another bad place is no solution. But that is exactly what they are doing now. Sooner or later they will discover Japan as their oasis. They will not swarm to our rural districts, for there is no room for them in Japan. They will come to our metropolitan areas, especially to Tokyo areas. Once they acquire the idea of coming to Japan, the number of emigrants will not be hundreds or thousands, but tens of thousands to hundreds of thousands a year. The economic, moral, and sociological impact upon Japan will indeed be far-reaching. Unless this situation is handled with a high degree of skill and wisdom, Japan will become disintegrated, and then there will be war—we could say, almost hell. The lazy and self-centered man in Japan will make an attempt to close his eyes and forget. When men such as this realize that they can no longer forget, they will make an endeavor to prevent this migration. If they find that they cannot prevent it, they will endeavor to postpone the day of its arrival. But in the end, they will fail. Reluctantly they will yield to this certain reality. This is a reflection of a weak man's philosophy of life. Why not look hard at the picture of what is bound to come! Why not decide that what is bound to come be welcomed?

A large-scale Asiatic migration to Japan could be a great blessing to Japan, Asia, and to the whole world if we view and handle the situation with faith, courage, and wisdom. As I stated earlier, we must believe in the fundamental equality of Man and in his capacity to adapt himself to any new environment. We must have the will to fight with difficulties. In other words, we should take courage and not be afraid of doing big things. We can do small matters easily. If we do something big, there is bound to be criticism, opposition, obstacles—even determined enemies who would destroy us. We should not be afraid. We should take courage and joy in doing battle against the array of forces such as these. We should have farsightedness. We should possess proper caution. We should maintain the sense of good order. Faith and courage go well together, as I have said, but if they are not supplemented with wisdom, we are bound to fail.

My proposal that a large-scale migration of Asiatic population to Japan be welcomed is not an alternative to the economic development of less-developed areas, nor is it an alternative to seeking more trade with less-developed areas. Instead, this proposal is made to help other men to develop Asia.

One serious bottleneck in the development of Asia is psychological and not material. It is complained that the same amount of capital and technological assistance given by Western countries to Japan and other Asiatic countries has brought about quite different results. Japan utilized her gifts and has made rapid progress. Other countries in Asia, with some notable exceptions, wasted theirs and enriched only a few people. The worst example is to be found in Indonesia. There, things are no better now than in its colonial period, except that Indonesia's people are more politically minded. In other regions of Asia aid policy has had exceedingly detrimental effects. The habit of receiving aid has created in the peoples of those countries a permanent dependence upon foreign aid. Moreover, the complaint continues, the receivers of foreign aid are not thankful as they should be to the givers, but on the contrary are more resentful of the donors than before they were given aid; foreign aid does not create international goodwill, as the original thought intended that it should, but instead it creates ill feelings and increases international frictions. I would say that such statements of the complainers may be exaggerated. With my very limited knowledge, I can point out hundreds of highly successful examples of foreign aid. I think that on the whole the foreign aid policy developed after World War II has been successful. On the other hand, we must frankly admit that there are many and serious limitations, even dangers, which we cannot afford to ignore. What is the root of the trouble?

I think that the root of the trouble concerning foreign aid in Asia is that our Asiatic brothers have not acquired the habits of utilizing it to their ultimate benefit. Under their long periods of colonial oppression they acquired the habits that people long oppressed and exploited do. Once they received aid, they spent it for their immediate purposes. In some countries that are overpopulated and have little room for work, labor is regarded as vice. In some places, religion and long-established customs are hindrances to economic development. It is easy to blame people, but blaming them does not bring about any good results.

It has been justifiably proposed that education is the foundation of healthy economic development. There is no question that this is true. Japan is the best example. Education should be encouraged, has in fact been encouraged, and it has been successful to some extent. However, we must admit also the negative side resulting from it. Unless means are found for providing educated people with good jobs, they are more discontented than when they were ignorant and they become the cause of social unrest. This unfortunate situation is happening all over Asia; so some people are becoming more or less skeptical about education as a means of solution. I do not share this skepticism. I think that education in Asia on the whole has been successful and has considerably helped to improve Asia in many respects. The negative factors complained about may be true; yet these negatives are but transitory and temporary situations. In the long run, this kind of dilemma will disappear. Still, I do not think that we can ignore the negative aspects of education. Although I am in favor of more, not less, education in Asia, I think that the negative side of education should be studied and a constructive solution found.

A large-scale migration of Asiatic population to Japan will change the habits of the emigrants. Regardless of their nationalities, they will soon acquire habits of working and saving as our ordinary Japanese people have. Given a new environment, it would be relatively easy for them to work with happiness; for man is made to work, and he is happy when he is provided opportunity to work. Most Asiatic emigrants to Japan will remain permanently in Japan. However, some of them at least will return to their countries to remain permanently or temporarily. These people will have a tremendous effect upon their own countries. In other words, an Asiatic migration to Japan would have an educational effect upon Asia and would indirectly help in its economic development. Of course, I am assuming that easy and cheap transportation between Japan and other Asiatic countries would be available. While the majority of emigrants would remain in Japan permanently, they would go back and forth frequently. And I would say, the more travel the better.

If what I am proposing does happen within thirty years or so, the population of the Tokyo area would not be the estimated 60 to 70 million, but 150 to 200 million. Could Tokyo's area absorb such a vast population? Obviously not. We would have to change our idea of Tokyo. If there is objection to using the name Tokyo, it would be a simple matter to change it. We might call it "Kanto" or "Tokaido," or whatever name which fit our or your feeling. However, it would not be practicable to distribute the whole of this migrant population equally to all parts of Japan. The population would be bound to be concentrated in some district. While I am in favor of creating new industrial cities in various parts of Japan, it is not an answer to the concentration to be expected. Tokyo is bound to be the center of Japan. In the Meiji and Taisho periods, Tokyo was Japan's political center, and Osaka was its industrial and commercial center. Tokyo has the distinct advantage of having the government as well as commerce and industry. So the weight is definitely on the side of Tokyo. Since World War II, Nagoya has grown considerably and has become a formidable rival of Osaka. The recent tendency is that all three of these metropolises—Tokyo, Osaka, and Nagoya—are being correlated and are becoming the real center of Japan. Although this is a vast area, the center of gravity will remain Tokyo. This area will have 150 to 200 million in population, including Japanese, Koreans, Chinese, Indians, Filipinos, and all other Asiatic peoples. There will be constant confusion, but I think that the tempo of amalgamation will be swift; so that in the long run, Tokyo will be a good community.

The effects of the Asiatic migration to Japan will be on the whole beneficial. It will tremendously increase our manpower, which now already has a shortage. With this vast industrious population, Japan will perhaps become the most powerful nation in the world. It will enrich Japanese thought and thinking. Although the origins of the Japanese may have been heterogeneous, they have been amalgamated for a long, long time and now are homogeneous. They are perhaps more homogeneous than any other peoples in the world. This has many advantages, such as the common language and the common tradition. However, we have reached the stage where we need more international understanding. In this respect, the fact that we are too homogeneous is a distinct disadvantage. Although we are great traders in the field of economy, we are quite provincial in thought and thinking. So a certain amount of confusion is necessary to make us realize that our ways of thinking are not always right. We must learn to live with people who have different ways of thinking and living than our own. Asiatic emigrants in Japan will have a good educational effect in this sense.

In making this proposal, I am, of course, assuming many things. Whatever the total population in 2000 may be, 7 per cent of the whole could not feed the total population. We must import food. It is a curious argument that a nation should be self-sufficient in its food production. If we must insist on being self-sufficient in food, why are we not insistent on being self-sufficient in fuel? Without fuel there would be no transportation, no industry, and in fact, no agriculture. The people would starve. As for fuel, we rely almost totally upon a foreign supply. We must abandon this old, traditional concept that a nation should be self-sufficient in food. Instead, we must develop agriculture in tropical zones. The cost of food would be cut almost by one-half of its present cost. As for transportation, some drastic measures would have to be taken. It is outmoded and unnecessary that individuals own and drive their own automobiles. We must reacquire our old custom of using public buses or subways. Perhaps it would be easy for us of Japan to give up our idea of owning and driving private cars, because the majority of our people still do not own them. New

York people already are beginning to disown automobiles. This tendency is healthy, and it is not too early for us to start a disown-cars movement.

In making this proposal, I am assuming that Communist China will change her belligerent attitude. I do not insist that China should give up communism. That is her own affair. What is more important for us is that China should mind her own affairs, rather than exporting revolutions. What I want from China is not the export of revolutions but the export of people. They are industrious and honest. They would have a good effect upon Japan, and China would be benefited also.

In making this proposal, I am assuming that the world will become more orderly under the leadership of the United Nations, so that the United Nations will help us in building the new Tokyo. My proposal is essentially Japanese and Asiatic, but it will have a tremendous effect upon the world. Thus, it is that Tokyo should be considered as a world problem. Japan and other Asiatic countries could not handle the Tokyo problem alone. We would need much capital and much technical assistance from advanced countries.

Lastly, in making this proposal, I am assuming that peoples, especially Asiatic peoples, will surrender their narrow construction of the meaning of nationalism, while firmly holding on to their true patriotism which lives within their spirits.

With all these assumptions being substantiated, Tokyo in the year 2000 would become the greater center of world civilization.

4

Victor L. Urquidi

The Underdeveloped City

Contemporary cities belong to poor people.
—J. F. C. Turner, at UN Interregional Seminar on Urban Development Planning and Policy, Pittsburgh, 1966.

The disintegration of Rome was the ultimate result of its overgrowth . . . a menacing example of uncontrolled expansion, unscrupulous exploitation, and materialistic repletion.
—Lewis Mumford, *The City in History*, 1961.

Contener el problema, evitando así que empeore.
—From a report, Inter-American Development Bank, 1965.

I.

Urban growth, occurring at a considerably higher rate than overall population growth, is rapidly gaining importance in the list of unsolved, and perhaps insoluble, social and economic problems of the less-developed countries of the world. Although in some of these nations there were clear signs of accelerated urbanization during the forties, particularly under the impact of World War II and its consequences, it is since 1950, approximately, that the process has gathered speed. But this process is still largely urban growth and not urban development, if the latter term is taken to mean an organic, purposeful pattern of change that may contribute to solid economic advance and greater well-being without creating painful imbalances or producing new forms of social ills. Cities, of different sizes and conditions, are growing. They hold more people, expand horizontally and vertically, concentrate more industrial and commercial activity in their midst, attract the major shares of investment and services, and benefit proportionately more than rural areas from educational and general cultural advancement. But growth of the cities in the poorer countries, unforeseen on its current scale, has brought a new dimension to social and economic development—the requirement that, somehow, economic growth, difficult in itself, be made compatible with desirable standards of urban life and take into account the many complex forces that shape the city and the behavior of its inhabitants.

The problems of urbanization are, of course, world-wide. The city is of great concern to sociologists, planners, statesmen and politicians, the news media, and ordinary people in the industrially developed nations of the world. Although the lurid descriptions of the industrial towns of the nineteenth century are largely a matter of history, today's economic wealth in the more advanced nations has not led to socially satisfactory solutions. Almost measureless contrasts remain between the living and housing conditions of the families in the upper income brackets and those in the underprivileged layers. Recent and sudden realization of those differences is demanding a serious reappraisal of urban development policies, and the consideration not only of the internal problems of each city, but of the interrelationships of urban centers among themselves and the ultilmate meaning of urbanization for a nation as whole.

The gravity of these problems in the developed countries of the Western world, and the almost frightening implications of the vast future megalopolitan conurbations in prospect, cannot be underestimated. However, most of the literature on the subject, whether gloomy or Utopian, treats the city, or the chain of cities, as amenable to some sort of concerted effort on the part of planners and authorities at local and national levels: resources are potentially available and what is needed, broadly, is decision in terms of social and political priority (aside from certain controversies between different exponents of town planning). In the less-developed parts of the world—where, it should not be forgotten, average per capita incomes vary in different regions from one-twentieth to one-fourth of the average incomes in the industrially advanced nations—the problem is one of virtual unavailability of resources, in addition to the far from simple decision-making aspect (on which the prospects may be incomparably less encouraging). Urbanization in the less-developed countries is necessary for modern development, but it is assuming some of the worst features of the growth of cities in the industrial nations and is being compounded by unprecedented social change stemming from high rates of population growth and massive movements of people from rural to urban areas.

All these circumstances are producing the *underdeveloped city*— the city of the underdeveloped nations. Because of the economic and political context in which it is evolving, this kind of city may well become the permanently underdeveloped city. The following is an attempt to survey the broad conditions surrounding this particular facet of the "Development Decade" and some of the lines of approach that may help to contain the problem, at least. I have drawn largely on recent literature on demographic change and urban development.[1] I cannot claim any specialized knowledge—which may be an advantage —but try to view the problem more generally, as a development economist may be likely to, though not to the point of allowing the whole picture to become blurred and dissolved in platitudes. I shall, inevitably, draw mainly on Latin American data and experience, but much of what emerges from this picture is probably applicable to urban growth in Asia and parts of Africa.

II.

Over 2.2 billion people inhabit the underdeveloped world, as against about one billion in the more economically fortunate countries. A common measure of the level of urbanization is the percentage of population living in towns of more than 20,000 inhabitants. This was 14 per cent in 1920, 19 per cent in 1940, and 25 per cent in 1960 for the world as a whole; that is fully 753 million people in 1960.[2] Of this amount, over one-half, some 380 million, lived in the less-developed areas: southern and eastern Asia, Latin America, and Africa.[3] In Latin America, the ratio inhabiting towns 20,000 and over in 1960 was 32 per cent, whereas it was only 14 per cent in southern Asia; in North America, it was 57 per cent, in Europe 41 per cent, and in the Soviet Union 36 per cent.[4] During 1940-1960, the number of inhabitants in such towns more than doubled in the less-developed areas: in Latin America, it rose by 170 per cent, in Africa by 164 per cent, in southern Asia by 130 per cent, and in eastern Asia by 96 per cent.[5] In the developed areas, these increases ranged from 24 to 76 per cent.

However, towns containing from 20,000 to 100,000 people cannot be taken as cities in the ordinary sense of the word. If cities holding 100,000 and over are taken as indicators of urbanization, the percentage of world population living in them rose from 8.6 per cent in 1920 to 12.6 per cent in 1940 and 17.5 per cent in 1960; there was a rise of 82 per cent from 1940 to 1960.[6] At present some 600 million persons live in cities this size, and perhaps one-half of them are in the less-developed countries, where rates of increase are generally higher.

Yet another convenient cut-off point is the 500,000 limit, which distinguishes large cities from mere cities and towns. By 1960, almost 12 per cent of the world's population, or 352 million people, inhabited such large cities, as against 5 per cent in 1920. In southern Asia, Latin America, and Africa, the number of inhabitants in cities of this rank more than tripled between 1940 and 1960 and rose by almost that rate in eastern Asia; it doubled in North America and the Soviet Union and went up only by one-fifth in Europe. The decade of the fifties, in particular, witnessed a more rapid expansion of the large towns and the metropolises than of the smaller cities. Urban concentration increased, especially in the Soviet Union and in the less-developed areas. In the latter regions, 46 per cent of the urban population in 1960 was already living in cities of 500,000 or more people. The rapidity with which this occurred in these regions does not, of course, mean that the levels of urbanization of the industrial countries were being reached, but it is significant that almost as many people lived in cities above 500,000 inhabitants in the poorer countries as in the richer.[7] In Latin America alone, 17 per cent of its total population in 1960 was in this type of city, a ratio higher than that of the other less-developed regions, equal to the European, and above the world average.[8]

Given differential rates of population increase between the developed and the underdeveloped areas, the latter (excluding Japan) are expected to account for over three-fourths of world population by the year 2000, assuming a total of 6.13 billion inhabitants.[9] It is estimated, in fact, that over 85 per cent of the increase in world population between 1965 and the year 2000 will take place in the less-developed areas,[10] owing to the expectation of high birth rates in these areas, assisted by declining mortality, as against the lower population growth trends prevailing in the industrial countries. Judging from recent trends and experience, and the many factors attracting people to the cities and inducing them to migrate from rural areas and small towns, it may be that by the year 2000 close to one-fourth of the world's total population will inhabit cities of 500,000 people and over; of these 1.5 billion persons, perhaps as many as two-thirds, or nearly one billion, will be in the less-developed regions. Out of this billion or so people, easily 300 million will be in Latin America. If the dividing line is put at 100,000, the less-developed areas may contain more than 1.8 billion inhabitants in cities of that size and over, of which some 400 million will be in Latin America.

Latin America seems to be taking the lead insofar as rates of increase are concerned, for nearly 47 per cent of its population may be living by the year 2000 in cities of 500,000 inhabitants and over, which would be almost twice the ratio for the world as a whole. And approximately 60 per cent of Latin America's future population is likely to inhabit cities with more than 100,000 inhabitants each. In 1960, already 19 Latin American cities had over half a million people; today there are at least 22 such cities, and there will be many more in the future as rural-urban migration continues and people flow from smaller to medium-sized towns and thence to the larger ones.

Rapid urbanization is evident throughout Latin America. Using the standard definition, for international comparisons, of 20,000 inhabitants and over as urban, Latin America's urban population expanded at an average annual rate of 5.1 per cent between 1940 and 1960. This rate was at least 5.3 per cent in 1950-1960. In this decade, in the two most populous countries, Brazil and Mexico, the rate was 6.5 and 5.2 per cent, respectively. In Venezuela, it was 8.2 per cent; in the Dominican Republic, a small country, it was 9.0 per cent; in Panama, 5.1 per cent. In Mexico, the growth rate of urban population in cities of 100,000 inhabitants and over, during 1950-1960, was 5.3 per cent; these cities accounted for two-thirds of all urban population in 1960. The corresponding rates in Venezuela and Brazil were 8.1 and 5.5 per cent.[11] In Venezuela, the number of people in cities having more than 100,000 inhabitants was only 10 per cent of total population in 1940, but this share had risen to 30 per cent by 1961.[12]

Some of the larger cities of Latin America increased their population during the 1950's by 60 to 70 per cent; for example, Mexico City, São Paulo, Bogotá, Guayaquil, Quito; and some almost doubled it or more, such as Caracas, Lima, Cali, Santo Domingo, Monterrey, Belo Horizonte, Guadalajara. Even higher rates of increase were recorded in certain smaller cities. Expansion was less rapid in Buenos Aires, the largest capital in Latin America, and Rio de Janeiro, former capital of Brazil, but in these two cities size itself is already significant, so that even a 3 per cent annual growth is important to reckon with.

Present trends in Latin America are likely to continue generally, although rates of urbanization may slow down in some of the larger countries as well as in the larger capitals. Rural-urban migration is not likely to abate, but may be directed increasingly to the medium-sized cities as industrial and commercial development spreads to them. A doubling of urban population as a whole every fifteen years is the minimum outlook, whereas rural population in the same time-span may rise by only 40 per cent (which in itself is disquieting). In countries such as Ecuador, Colombia, and some of the Central American nations, expansion will be threefold every fifteen years, and in others, such as the Dominican Republic and Venezuela, four- to fivefold, if present trends continue.[13]

Data on world population, especially for the less-developed areas, are subject to revision and should, of course, be taken as estimates. Approximations are even larger in the case of urban population, for which there are different definitions, and a given-sized town in terms of number of inhabitants obviously has quite a different meaning in Africa than in Latin America. Projections to the year 2000 are, furthermore, no better than the assumptions on which they are based. Nevertheless, it seems necessary to have some idea of magnitudes, not only important in themselves but also as background to other considerations affecting urban growth and giving it peculiar features in our time.

III.

The rapidly growing Latin American cities—and the same is broadly true in the other less-developed areas—are not the product of highly productive agricultural and industrial societies, but are associated with conditions where rural productivity is usually low, manufacturing is only partially developed, the levels of education, skills, health, and welfare are still grossly inadequate, and income and property are highly concentrated. Latin America's cities—even the larger ones of European vintage—are poor; poor and partially run-down, or poor and backward, or poor on the average with splashes of wealth interspersed in shockingly grim slums and ugly surroundings, held together by increasingly inadequate transportation and other services. Latin American nations are beset with the "premature city"—a preview of a future "noncity" if current development prospects remain unchanged.

It is common knowledge that in almost every large city of Latin America, so-called "marginal" communities have sprung up around it, or have sometimes penetrated into its heart. They vary from shanty-towns to squatter settlements and clandestine subdivisions, and constitute what one author terms uncontrolled urban settlements, largely inevitable.[14] These settlements are or have been the "reception centers," by and large, for the poor and unskilled migrants from the rural areas and the lesser urban zones. The expansion of these communities has been so rapid and unexpected that it has been impossible to supply them with essential services—water, sewerage, light, and the other usual municipal services; they lack schools, health units, protection, and amenities; the land on which they are settled is frequently subject to flooding and erosion; their housing consists largely of hovels ingeniously contrived from waste metal, wood, stone, or board; they sometimes have a "civic" organization of their own, but they also all too frequently harbor the habitual criminals and breed violence, theft, and vice. To these areas must be added the traditional hard-core city slums, perhaps worsened today. Slum dwellers and marginal community dwellers may number from one-quarter to one-half or more of the population of the larger cities in India, Turkey, Peru, Venezuela, Iraq, Senegal, and many other countries.

These squatter subcities of squalor are the result of two main difficulties: on the one hand, the inability of rural areas to provide a living to a rapidly increasing population; on the other, the incapacity of the economic system to absorb urban dwellers sufficiently into industrial employment.[15] Both sets of problems require some elaboration, and through them runs a third factor, namely, relatively high levels of fertility combined with declining general and child mortality, which for the time being means unprecedented rates of growth of population that are likely to be sustained for a long period of time.[16]

Rural conditions are in most countries responsible for a large share of the migration to squatters' settlements in the larger towns. In spite of progress in many areas, the land tenure systems are inadequate and frequently socially unjust. Most farmers do not own land, or they have such small plots, freehold or in rental, that they cannot make a living. Programs to improve farming methods and raise yields, to broaden markets, and otherwise to provide incentives have been insufficient. People move to urban centers not because new techniques have made them redundant on the farms, as in the advanced countries, but because the land cannot feed them. They go in search of better-paid occupations, new opportunities or the apparent security—or even the "lure"—of the city. It would not be possible here to analyze these problems in detail. There is a growing awareness of them, and many agrarian and farm development programs are under way in Latin America, India, Pakistan, and elsewhere. But it is doubtful that the scale of these programs is large enough. And it must be admitted that, insofar as they succeed, the logical conclusion, as productivity and incomes rise, would be for more people to move to nonagricultural occupations. It would help if new manufacturing industries were established in areas where there is a surplus farm population, around the smaller towns.

Industrial development, largely and necessarily confined to the cities, has not yet reached a stage where it is broadly enough based to cope with the potential additions to the industrial labor force arising from migration into the cities, or even to absorb the natural growth of urban population in the working ages. It has been found that in 1960 the share of manufacturing employment in total nonagricultural employment in Latin America was 27 per cent as against 35 per cent twenty years earlier, and that employment in tertiary activities is relatively higher in the region than it was in Europe or the United States at a similar stage of industrialization.[17] This means that employment in trade and services and the many lesser occupations has increased in Latin America more rapidly than in industry, thus suggesting that the flow of migrants into the cities has resulted in a spread of urban under-employment. One estimate indicates that as many as 8.2 million people—12 per cent of the labor force—were in a condition of "disguised unemployment" in Latin America in 1960, and that instead of diminishing, this unproductive and subsistence-income sector of urban life may be expected to reach close to 11 million people by 1970.[18] In some countries, underemployment is estimated to be as high as 25 per cent of total employment in "miscellaneous services," which comprise a considerable slice of tertiary activity.[19]

Industrial development, despite high rates and spectacular advances in certain branches in the Latin American countries, is not yet rapid or diverse enough, nor are the supporting educational and training services in turn expanding adequately to absorb into steady and productive employment the additions to urban population in the working ages. Particularly, there are large surpluses of unskilled labor, including potentially employable female workers. Modern technological developments tend furthermore, in many cases, to increase the capital/labor ratios and, in any event, to require highly skilled personnel. Again, it would not be possible here to attempt any further analysis of the industrial development picture, except to say that in addition to the limited domestic markets, largely resulting from low farm productivity, there are numerous other problems connected with industrial and trade conditions, and generally, with the patterns and fluctuations of world trade, which affect unfavorably the development programs and policies of the poorer nations.

The imbalance between agricultural and industrial productivity and the difficulty in pursuing both adequate agricultural development and more rapid industrial growth are thus at the heart of the expansion of marginal and squatter communities in the Latin American cities. These people are there and they are increasing in numbers. According to one estimate, such "marginal groups" grow at rates of as much as 15 per cent annually in some places.[20] This creates pressure not only on employment but on wages, and tends to cheapen labor below subsistence levels. It further establishes an impossible burden on urban facilities, and constitutes an increasing source of political instability. Thus living conditions in the cities reflect—and will long continue to do so—the economic plight not only of their inhabitants but of the underdeveloped economies as a whole.

Adequate city growth, housing, and services can only be the product of high productivity and rapidly rising output combined with an efficient educational system, an equitable tax structure, better income distribution, a less rigid social structure, and a careful awareness of the totality of factors affecting the city. The expansion of the middle-income strata in the developing countries, though it creates a demand for much of what a modern city should be, hardly offsets the growing weight of the supply of entrants into the marginal communities. Thus for every middle-class apartment building or office skyscraper, there may arise overnight thousands of hovels inhabited by five, six, or more persons per room. These are uneducated, hungry, unhealthy and needy persons, who have few opportunities for social and economic advancement. According to one study, 90 per cent of migrants into Santiago, Chile, fail to develop any upward mobility.[21] Innumerable examples may be given of unemployment, low income, and appalling living conditions in squatter settlements in Latin American and elsewhere.[22]

IV.

Apart from the increasing sprawl of the underdeveloped city, the grotesque transportation systems, the noise and the now rapidly spreading air pollution, the lack of water, the flooding, the almost totally absent police, the filth, and the unsightly, unplanned building agglomerations, one major problem stands out: housing. It has been argued that the urban housing problem in the less-developed countries is insoluble. This is easily an intuitive and *a priori* statement that many would question. However, it may be not far off the mark. Recent estimates for Latin America—and no doubt similar calculations have been made for other areas—indicate that the approximately seven-million-unit shortage in urban housing, even in terms of the presently inadequate definitions, could be proportionately reduced—that is, in relation to total housing needs—within this century, but not eliminated.[23]

Present rates of construction of dwellings are on the whole low. In 1964, one estimate indicated construction of slightly over 400,000 units, urban and rural, which is two new dwelling units per thousand inhabitants. Another estimate suggests the ratio might have been three.[24] Mexico, Venezuela, and Brazil are particularly lagging in meeting new annual housing needs. Chile, Costa Rica, and Columbia may be near to facing the yearly increase in requirements. It is unlikely that, despite new programs and new domestic and external sources of finance, much headway has been made beyond the 1964 rates. It is therefore doubtful that the shortage is being reduced. To merely keep the deficit from rising, assuming minimal average space per dwelling unit, Latin America would have to build annually several times as many units as at present; perhaps some six times the present rate of construction, resulting in a ratio of ten units per thousand inhabitants. To do this, the annual investment cost, conservatively estimated (including utilities and basic facilities), would equal almost 40 per cent of the present rate of aggregate gross investment (which is about 16 per cent of GNP).[25] Given certain conditions, this might not be out of the question, but certainly extremely difficult. It would still mean carrying forward indefinitely the seven-million urban deficit, as well as the rural shortage (variously estimated between 8 and 14 million units). To actually reduce the deficit, at least that in cities, would of course require a much greater effort and a larger share of gross investment annually.[26] One could speculate about various financial possibilities and assumptions about growth rates, saving ratios, tax burdens, housing specifications, and so forth. But it is only necessary to recall that besides urban housing (and rural), there are other tasks to be performed—in education, land tenure, agricultural development, health and welfare, and other urgent social and economic needs in Latin America and elsewhere.

The problem, obviously, is not one of financial or even real resources only, much less one that can be helped much by international financial cooperation. It is also one of basic concepts. "A passive attitude is generally adopted in the face of the progressive aggravation of the shortage of housing and community services, and there is a tendency to concentrate on the ornamental aspects of town planning."[27] But town planning itself, in the sense of operating plans rather than architects' dreams, is almost nonexistent. Where a city has been planned and developed from scratch, as in the case of Brasilia, it has solved little or nothing. Housing development suffers, in consequence, from the inadequacy of overall planning. Ad hoc solutions prevail, and even the best housing programs run into difficulties and prove inadequate to the scale of the city's problems.

For these reasons also, the design of housing and urban community programs is unrealistic in terms of the forces influencing urban development. Most public and other housing programs in the less-developed countries are in effect attempting to meet, at best, the requirements of certain types of middle-class demand, and even in the lower middle strata the standards and materials used tend to be those of the richer countries. Housing costs are high in relation to the level of development and purchasing power. A mere comparison of labor and materials costs between, say, California and Asunción, Paraguay, is simply beside the point, for in fact in the latter country such costs, though lower, may be higher in terms of wage-income and of prospective real income. Interest on housing loans is generally higher in the less-developed countries, both absolutely and relatively.

Closely related to this is the question of land values. The estimates for the cost of housing programs in Latin America, merely to contain the problem, make little allowance for the actual cost of land. In the case of a minimal housing unit, in a multifamily four-storied building, with an average of 80 square meters of land per unit of 70 square meters of floor-space, the cost of land and basic services would be at least 9 per cent of the total unit-cost; for a middle-income family, it would vary from one-tenth for 80 square meters of floor-space to one-fifth for twice that amount of construction per unit.[28] Land values in Latin American cities are notoriously high, as a result of speculation, investment preferences, lack of regulation, and general economic factors. In one Latin American capital, Caracas, site values in different parts of the city increased from 4 to 18 times in a thirteen-year period.[29] "There is today no supply of land in Caracas within the reach of low- and middle-income families, and even undeveloped land prices are so high that they have become prohibitive for utilization in low-cost housing."[30] It is common in Latin American cities for middle- and low-income families to have to pay more for the site than for the dwelling-unit built on it. In most Latin American countries, according to the Inter-American Development Bank, there are considerable legal and other difficulties in purchasing land for housing projects, aside from the cost.

Public housing programs should imply adequate institutional arrangements, ranging from a basic law, research services, and coordination of the work of the various agencies within an overall plan, to appropriate relationships to other aspects of urban and regional development. In most Latin American countries, such arrangements are seriously deficient. Merely on the side of efficiency in construction and research on new materials and cost-reducing methods, the situation is poor. Except for seven or eight countries undertaking such research, the rest of the Latin American countries continue to build with old-fashioned methods.[31]

Given the prevailing income-distribution in most less-developed countries, a large majority of potential householders would in any event be unable to pay, within a reasonable period, for both house and land, or even for construction alone. It is not clear to what extent efforts to reduce the cost per dwelling unit would actually meet the weak levels of demand at market prices and under ordinary financing conditions. Low-cost housing projects frequently suffer from rapid turnover in occupancy because of nonpayment, and owners or tenants are apt to overcrowd their dwellings and turn them partly to commercial uses.

An adequate consideration of the housing problem cannot, therefore, abstract from general economic conditions or from the social, cultural, and technological framework. A merely quantitative approach is insufficient, however attainable the quantitative goals may appear to be. The housing problem seems to raise serious doubts about urban life in general, but the latter is in turn largely a reflection of inadequate economic development coupled with unduly high population growth. The answer to urban development, and the future of the presently underdeveloped city, must be sought, consequently, in the broader context of economic growth and social change, rather than in the city itself or in its structure.

V.

In the industrially advanced nations there is a fairly purposeful and concentrated effort to apply knowledge and organizational ability to the expansion of output and to the extension of the benefits of productivity to the mass consumer; this is true under different social systems, including the Soviet. The less-developed nations as a whole do not appear to be catching up with the industrial countries. They are induced by modern communications—advertising, radio and TV, cinema, and periodicals—to adopt the aspirations and the consumption patterns of the high-income countries. They also partially incorporate up-to-date technology into many activities, all too often without regard for local conditions in the labor market that favor labor-intensive rather than capital-intensive industry. Within fragmented and discontinuous domestic markets, frequently small, they permit unhampered and irrational private investment decisions to be made that lead to high-cost manufacturing and low manpower absorption. Educational and other social programs are inadequate and are held back by economic progress itself. World trade conditions are not favorable to the less-developed countries, and international attitudes to development, in spite of much good talk—for instance, at the United Nations, at regional summit meetings, and other gatherings—can only be called begrudging at best. The international political situation is no less discouraging as the nuclear and space-age powers involve the poorer nations in their rivalries. Development under these conditions will be a miracle indeed. And the cities can only be a part of that whole, not a separate entity. Urban development can only begin to be rational in response to an improvement in the general conditions favoring growth and social change.

It is said that most so-called solutions to the urban development problems are not more than short-term partial answers to inadequately defined issues. Much research is needed to help achieve better evaluations on which to base policies. But, as in most other aspects of development, policies have to be established even in the absence of full and adequate information and analysis. Above all, as many have pointed out, a "strategy" needs to be adopted. There cannot be partial answers, nor can successful projects of a particular country be transplanted wholesale to another. It is often the planner—using this term in a broad sense—who makes attainment of a plan impossible, because he sets his aim too high or tries to reach too many objectives at the same time. This is particularly the case with urban planning, where social and even aesthetic considerations may cloud the economic reality. But it is also the lack of overall vision that repeatedly prevents individual programs from succeeding or from leading the way to broader solutions.

It seems necessary, in the underdeveloped countries, to recognize certain conditioning factors that are not likely to change for some time. Thus any policies adopted should duly take them into account. Population growth, even with intensified family planning programs, is bound to continue at a high rate, and rural-urban migration can be expected to put increasing pressure on urban facilities. The expansion of cities is unquestionably a necessary condition of industrialization, and industrial growth is the main instrument by which development can be accelerated and social mobility increased. But given the nature and level of the physical and human resources of a less-developed country and the effective educational opportunities likely to arise, a broad policy should set out to impede the sort of concentration that is now taking place in the larger cities. The poorer countries are economically and institutionally unprepared for such concentration. An essential piece of the strategy should thus be to encourage the growth of the smaller cities through the spread of manufacturing and other modern activities by means of appropriate incentives and suitable regional planning. Until recently, inadequate communications were a potent force tending to concentrate industry in the capital cities or other large towns. But modern methods of transportation are bringing about new location patterns. This process needs to be stimulated, as a means of slowing down or spreading out the rural-urban migration and avoiding the high social costs of excessive urbanization, and also of raising incomes in the smaller urban centers to the level where housing and other improvements can come within partial reach of the local market. Such a policy will not slow down urbanization as a whole, but will at least avoid high concentration.

Meanwhile, given certain perhaps unduly skeptical assumptions about present trends in social progress in the less-developed countries, some aspects of urban reality must be faced squarely. Marginal low-income groups will exist for a long time; they will be increased by rural-urban migration and by high birth-rates; they cannot be regarded as temporary or as if they were about to become conventional middle-class strata. Urban development plans must therefore allow for their gradual and selective improvement and incorporation. This part of the strategy is beginning to be recognized in many quarters and has in some countries become explicit. There are various means of giving it content. Slum clearance, as in the industrially advanced countries, is only applicable in the hard-core poorer areas of the large cities, but not in the so-called uncontrolled urban settlements or marginal communities. The existence of the latter and of the conditions creating them cannot be ignored. It therefore seems necessary to adapt certain institutions to their existence and to introduce in those settlements important elements of improvement in which the settlers may actively participate.

In many cases, it would be advisable to legalize "squatters' rights," particularly where the settlement is more than a place of temporary abode and shows clear symptoms of "progressiveness," as measured by occupational characteristics of its inhabitants, attitudes to ownership, and participation in community activity. Establishment of legal ownership should be accompanied by the subsidized introduction of basic municipal services, frequently with local participation in their construction through voluntary work. Subsidized cooperative programs for the sale of materials, free technical advice on building, and assistance in bettering conditions in the home and in family life are essential requirements of such programs. There have been many such experiments in Latin America, Africa, and Asia, including some in which "core houses" are provided to be expanded gradually. The "roof-loan" scheme in Ghana, the self-help projects in Santiago and Bogotá, and many others of a related nature seem to be steps in the right direction. All assume that the squatter is capable of organized activity and of a good measure of responsible behavior. "Squatting . . . is not to be understood as a totally lamentable phenomenon. . . . In some respects . . . the squatter enterprise is probably the most significant form of home-building taking place in the world today."[32] There thus seems to be a large volume of untapped savings, in the sense of potential effort, among the squatters, so that public resources may properly be put to work in that area.[33]

Legalization of squatters' rights may frequently require outright purchase of the land by a local authority, through a nationally financed program, in order to grant it to the squatter. In some cases, a subsidized sale would be preferable, or a combination of tenancy and sale over a given period of time. Each scheme would have to adapt to the particular characteristics of the settlement. A slightly different situation arises where the marginal community dwellers actually own, or have begun to pay for, the land they occupy and have started building on it. The need here would be for introduction of utilities and help in rationalizing the process of construction and development, and especially for replacement of onerous or inadequate financing by a suitable subsidized scheme, adapted to the actual and prospective income levels of the dwellers.

A strategy must also include consideration of the broad problem of land values, the incidence of which, even on the middle-income groups, is unduly unfavorable. The shift from run-down housing or a hovel into a better neighborhood or a moderate-income development may frequently be delayed or put off indefinitely by the influence of the site value on rentals or on the purchase price of the new dwelling. Given prevailing high rates of interest on ordinary housing loans and relatively short amortization periods, the would-be house-owner in an underdeveloped country is at a considerable disadvantage. There seems to be a need for strict regulation of urban sites and of the holding of undeveloped urban property, if speculative values are to cease to restrict housing development. The rise in site values, for instance, in Latin America, has virtually eliminated millions of people from the housing market and reduced the scope of innumerable housing projects. It has also contributed to the spread of unregulated settlements. It appears fundamental that some sort of "urban reform" parallel in many ways to land reform should be worked out. A combination of a drastic capital gains tax on urban properties in excess of a minimum value and regulations to prevent accumulation of urban wealth in private hands, and especially concentration of private property in low-income urban zones, would appear to be inevitable in the coming years. To be effective, urban reform would also have to place some restriction on indiscriminate private sales by holders of subsidized housing.

A new approach to problems of urban development would also seem to call for a revision of taxation of urban property in general, especially in order to introduce the principle of progressive rates. Costly modern suburban development expenditures for the upper middle-class in Latin American cities should be offset by high local rates and special assessments, and, in general, large wealthy-quarter estates, often involving extensive sites, should be subject to effective assessment and progressive rates. Urban property taxes in large Latin American cities, where tax capacity is relatively higher among certain groups, are in effect low, and even nominally low.

The effective rate of the Mexican property tax on urban property is approximately one-half of 1 per cent of true or fair market value, compared with the nominal rate of 1.09 per cent of appraised value. . . . The nominal tax rate in Caracas is 6 per cent of potential rents; in Montevideo it is 0.65 per cent of appraised value (excluding surtax) . . . [but] effective rates must have been only a small fraction of nominal rates. The heavier effective rate in Mexico results mostly from better administration rather than higher nominal rates. [However], revenue from the property tax is approximately [only] 1 per cent of national income originating in the Federal District [of Mexico], about twice the share found in Caracas, but less than half the share found in American cities with populations of one million or more. . . . Mexican property tax rates . . . are modest by comparison with rates in most American cities, and, in fact, with prevailing rates in many jurisdictions where the level of economic development is no higher than in the Federal District of Mexico.[34]

Thus there is ample room for further increases in effective rates, and there is no really valid reason for not introducing progressive rates, although some expert fiscal opinion stands for maintaining proportionality.[35]

Taxation and regulation of urban site values, and the broader policy of urban reform, should be regarded in the more general context of the reality of the extensive marginal communities, for which new expenditure priorities now seem to be indicated. Urban reform may be socially desirable generally, as a measure towards a more egalitarian society, but it is particularly needed as a part of a rational scheme for urban development, before the large underdeveloped cities are engulfed by squatter settlements and the ideal of a "green belt" around the large towns is substituted by a "brown belt" or a "filth belt," as is already beginning to be evident in many parts of the world. Authorizations to build expensive homes in middle-class suburbia should, in the interests of the owners themselves, be restricted or conditioned upon contributions to the financing of squatter developments or other schemes in the lower-income zones and to the improvement of substandard housing. The underdeveloped city cannot afford millionaire homes and millions of hovels side by side.

Technological innovation for the underdeveloped city is needed. Much technical progress in urban planning and in construction relates to what the wealthy communities of the industrially advanced nations are able to do in their own terms. Urban planning concepts, like industrial technology, would appear to require adaptation to the less-developed framework. Frequently, the proposals of urban planners, rich in imagination and humanistic ideals, are devoid of economic content; they are insufficiently related to the starting conditions or to the actual social possibilities of implementation, and they fail to quantify the many variables involved in bringing about results, nor do they take into account broader economic alternatives. Urban planning is part of a process; by itself it is necessarily incomplete. Closer association with economists and sociologists concerned with urban development is indispensable, for a totality of economic and social factors must come into the picture. In particular, the economics of the under-developed city, as distinct from the rich city of the Western industrial nations, must be made the object of careful study, and the whole interrelationship of urban development and overall economic and social development needs to be clarified.

Greater awareness of these problems in the less-developed countries is bound to lead to the adoption of national policies of urban development, in which suitable machinery may be set up to bring the growth and housing policies of the major cities under the scope of central or federal authorities, without restricting in any way the local functions or restraining local initiative. The industrial nations are moving in this direction, and much of the concern of planners now has to do with urban development as an integral part of national development. The less-developed countries, in view of their demographic prospects and their trends in urbanization, outlined earlier, are in equal need of national policies, if not more so. Urban growth, industrialization and regional planning can hardly be conceived today as separate processes. The expansion and modernization of transportation, both within cities and between them, has to be part and parcel of the same process and the same policies. New priorities in public expenditure, reflecting these objectives, are urgently needed in the poorer countries.

The underdeveloped cities are often projected into the future not on the basis of what they are and are likely to be, given their basic present conditions, or on the basis of a realistic process of change, but according to the models of the already outmoded cities of the industrially developed nations. This occurs equally in the latter nations, where policy-makers "have occasionally been trying to solve the problems of the city that was."[36] It must be conceded that any prognostication is risky, but most projections tend to be conservative in the extreme. Projections based on present conditions can be overly pessimistic. "Sociologists and economists who base their projects for future economic and urban expansion on the basis of forces now at work, projecting only such changes as may result from speeding up such forces, tend to arrive at a universal megalopolis, mechanized, standardized, effectively dehumanized, as the final goal of urban evolution."[37] This urban doomsday is not yet the outlook of sociologists, economists, or urban planners in the less-developed areas—if anything, they show insufficient awareness of the implications of urbanization—but there is certainly a built-in projection of present conditions. A recently published master plan for Monterrey, Mexico, where population is estimated to grow from the present one million to over five million by the year 2000, fails to consider any alternative to the private automobile and bus as a means of internal transportation, although the plan is well-conceived in most respects.[38] But, will automobiles as we now know them really be necessary by the year 2000? Even a city subway system may be obsolete by then. Urban development experts need not immerse themselves in science fiction, but alternative reasonable assumptions may easily be introduced in the projections.

There is clearly a need to increase knowledge of the present situation of cities in the underdeveloped nations. It is no less essential to reappraise the outlook, to work out revised approaches and policies, to try to achieve a new understanding, by all sectors, of the complex issues of tomorrow. Urban areas will benefit from overall economic and social development, but their own healthy development can be a positive contribution in turn to achievement of the broader objectives. The bleak prospect which, for lack of adequate policies, is now in sight is a proliferation of underdeveloped cities; it certainly calls for change. Ultimately, we are dealing not with land and concrete, or freeways, housing projects and community centers, or with water, parks or smog, but with people—human beings who must live and work together, who may aspire to be alone together, and who are unfortunately in the habit of multiplying (together) to an extent hitherto unforeseen.

NOTES

1. Among the particularly valuable sources, the following may be mentioned: Papers presented by the United Nations Population Division, other related bodies and individual experts to the UN Interregional Seminar on Urban Development Planning and Policy, Pittsburgh, October-November 1966; papers presented to the World Population Conference, Belgrade, September 1965; Luis Lander and Julio César Funes, "Urbanismo y desarrollo," in *Hacia una política de integración para el desarrollo de la América Latina*. Proceedings of the Sixth Inter-American Planning Congress, Caracas, November 6-11, 1966 (San Juan, Puerto Rico, Inter-American Planning Society, 1967), pp. 60-110; and Rubén D. Utría, "The Housing Problem in Latin America in Relation to Structural Factors in Development" in *Economic Bulletin for Latin America*, XI (October 1966) (United Nations, ECLA), pp. 81-110.

2. UN Population Division, *Trends in World Urbanization, 1920-1960*, paper submitted to the Interregional Seminar mentioned in footnote 1; derived from Table 2.

3. An apparently stricter definition of "less-developed areas" estimates only 321 million in this group in 1960, that is, 42.4 per cent of the total. This grouping presumably excludes Japan, where the degree of industrialization and urbanization is much higher and the rate of demographic increase much lower than in most other Asian countries, although per capita income is below Western levels. However, the subdivision of the 321 million by region is not available, and for this reason the higher figure is used in the text. (Cf. *ibid.*, Table 11.)

4. *Ibid.*, Table 4.

5. For these four regions as a whole the increase was 116 per cent; under the stricter definition (see footnote 3), it was 138 per cent. *(Ibid.,* Tables 2 and 11.)

6. *Ibid.*, derived from Table 1.

7. *Ibid.*, Tables 7-9. The stricter definition of "less-developed areas" reduces the share of the latter in the aggregate population of cities 500,000 and over to 39.5 per cent, and the ratio of inhabitants in these cities to total urban population to 43 per cent (Table 11).

8. *Ibid.*, Table 9. About 25 per cent was in cities of 100,000 and over.

9. Medium projection. Cf. John D. Durand, *"The Modern Expansion of World Population,"* Proceedings of the American Philosophical Society, CXI (June 1967), Table 1.

10. *Ibid.*, Table 5.

11. Data for Brazil from John Durand and César Peláez, "Patterns of Urbanization in Latin America," *Milbank Memorial Fund Quarterly*, XLIII (Part 2, October 1965), Tables 4 and 5. Data for Mexico, Venezuela, Panama and Dominican Republic from Carmen Miró, "The Population of Latin America," *Demography*, I (No. 1, 1964), Table 8.

12. Lander and Funes, *loc. cit.,* Table 13.

13. R. Utría, *loc. cit.*

14. J. F. C. Turner, *Uncontrolled Urban Settlements,* paper submitted to the Interregional Seminar cited in footnote 1. This paper contains an excellent analysis of the problems involved, with examples from many parts of the less-developed world. See also R. Utría, *loc. cit.*

15. R. Utría, *loc. cit. et passim,* and UN Population Division with the collaboration of Prof. Sidney Goldstein, *Urbanization and Economic and Social Change,* Interregional Seminar cited in footnote 1.

16. A survey conducted in seven Latin American capitals showed an average number of live-born children per woman of childbearing age ranging from 2.25 in Rio de Janeiro to 3.27 in Mexico City (leaving out Buenos Aires, where it was 1.49). Cf. Carmen Miró, "Some misconceptions disproved: a program of comparative fertility surveys in Latin America," in B. Berelson (ed.), *Family Planning and Population Programs* (Chicago, 1966), p. 639, Table 2.

17. Economic Commission for Latin America, *El proceso de industrialización en America Latina,* Anexo Estadístico, Santiago, Chile, 1966, pp. 11 and 13.

18. From B. Hopenhayn, *Ocupación y desarrollo económico en América Latina,* ILPES, Santiago, 1966, quoted by F. H. Cardoso and J. L. Reyna, *Industrialization, Occupational Structure and Social Stratification in Latin America,* in Cole Blasier (ed.), *Constructive Change in Latin America,* University of Pittsburgh Press, 1968, footnote 11, p. 54.

19. *Ibid.* p. 44.

20. Felipe Herrera, President of the Inter-American Bank, in a speech at the University of Salvador, Bahia, Brazil, Sept. 23, 1967.

21. Centro Latinoamericano de Demografía, *Encuesta sobre inmigración en el Gran Santiago,* quoted by Teresa Orrego Lyon, "Algunas consideraciones sobre marginalidad urbana," *Temas del BID,* Inter-American Development Bank, Washington, IV (September 1967), p. 30.

22. R. Utría, *loc. cit., passim,* quotes several; see also papers presented at Interregional Seminar, Pittsburgh, cited in footnote 1. A recent interesting comparative study of Latin American slums may be found in Lloyd H. Rogler, ."Slum Neighborhoods in Latin America," *Journal of Inter-American Studies,* IX (October 1967), pp. 507-528.

23. R. Utría, *loc. cit.,* pp. 96-97.

24. Both estimates are quoted in a thoughtful review of the question recently published by the Banco Francés e Italiano para América del Sur, "El problema de la vivienda en América Latina," *Estudios Economicos,* I (1967), pp. 49-67. The ratio per thousand inhabitants in Western Europe was 7.4 in 1961.

25. R. Utría, *loc. cit.,* p. 97.

26. The source quoted in footnote 24 contains alternative calculations by various authors. The problem still remains insoluble.

27. R. Utría, *loc. cit.*

28. *Ibid.,* p. 86, Table 1. It should be emphasized that these are data used as averages in a "planned" solution to the housing shortage. Ordinarily, land values are a higher proportion of total cost, especially for middle-class one-family housing, where they may reach as much as 50 per cent or more.

29. Lander and Funes, *loc. cit.*

30. *Ibid.,* p. 98.

31. From an Inter-American Development Bank report.

32. From "Profile" on Charles Abrams, in *The New Yorker,* 1967.

33. Improvements in squatters' settlements could also take the form of certain "collective" services to offset the need for provisional or partial housing, or narrow minimum space standards. I have in mind such things as dormitories, communal kitchens, baths,

laundries, children's areas, recreation clubs, and so on, which have been tried out in many places.

34. Oliver Oldman et al., *Financing Urban Development in Mexico City* (Cambridge, Mass.: Harvard University Press, 1967), pp. 79-80. The reference is to places in Africa, Brazil, and India.

35. The authors of the previously quoted book come out strongly *against* progressive rates. Cf. *ibid.*, p. 81.

36. Lowdon Wingo, Jr., "Urban Space in a Policy Perspective," in L. Wingo, Jr., ed., *Cities and Space—The Future Use of Urban Land* (Baltimore: The Johns Hopkins Press, 1962), p. 4.

37. Lewis Mumford, *The City in History* (New York: Harcourt, Brace and World, 1961), p. 527.

38. Departamento del Plan Regulador de Monterrey, N. L. y Municipios Vecinos, *El Plan Director de la Subregión Monterrey* (Monterrey: Dirección General de Planificación [Gobierno del Estado de Nuevo León], 1967).

5

Peter Hall

The Urban Culture and the Suburban Culture

There is a common notion: that economically, socially, culturally, and physically the urban areas of developed industrial nations become more and more alike. In Europe we hear constantly of the Americanization of London, of Paris, of Rome; while the German cities, by dint of wartime devastation and Marshall Aid, are thought to represent the case of instant Americanization.

Now it is true that there are profound changes, which are common to all urban areas of the Western world. By any standards of measurement we have, all great urban areas in Western nations, and most less-great ones too, are increasing more or less rapidly in population. More and more people are classed as urban, at least until a stage is reached, as in England, where so many are urban that the process can hardly continue. Associated with this, there is a marked and rapid shift of the work force out of agriculture and mining into manufacturing and above all into the service industries. Competition for space in city centers, coupled with constant growth of people and jobs, forces a re-sorting of economic and social patterns: more and more people, more and more jobs move to suburban locations increasingly far from the central business district, which only sixty years ago was the only important center of economic activity. More and more agricultural land is used up for low-density, single-family housing; and this even in countries, such as France and Germany, once thought to be pre-serves of the city apartment block.

And yet these underlying demographic, social, and economic changes are accompanied by remarkably different physical expressions. The transatlantic traveler is still amazed, even shocked, by the contrast between the modern North American urban landscape and the mod-ern northwest European. If he travels west, he will be nonplussed by the scale of the development, by the apparently endless sprawl of suburbs in the east coast megalopolis, by the vast network of freeways which links them, forming the first distinctive feature of the landscape visible from his vantage point seven miles up in the air. If he travels east, he will be surprised by the puniness of the development, by its toytown-like quality, by the planned precision that marks the geo-metrical break between town and country, by the apparent absence of agricultural collapse in the fringes around the developments. All this will be true, whether he travels over England, or the Netherlands, or Federal Germany, or Scandinavia.

For this surprising physical difference, there must be profound political, and therefore in the last resort cultural, reasons. In this paper I wish to explore the nature of the differences, their causes, and some of their implications for future planning in the two continents. I pro-pose to draw a distinction between two cultures, two basic notions of urbanism, which I think are characteristic of the two continents. Necessarily, this typology will contain a large measure of exaggeration because it will attempt to isolate central ideals, which are found only in diffused or mixed form on the ground. But I hope to show that it is important for our understanding of urban growth, and of our ideas about planning this growth, on both sides of the Atlantic.

On the one side, therefore, we have the European idea of urbanism. This is easy to define. It is the statement of the traditional *urban culture*. It holds that during five thousand years of European civilization, cities have achieved a special position in fostering and housing that civilization; that cities, as ancient repositories of culture, should be protected from decay; that urbanity, in the strict sense, is a virtue that should be preserved by the planner; that cities are organically related to the agricultural hinterlands around them, and that this relationship, too, should be preserved; that the social contacts between men and their neighbors are a central feature of urban civilization and are to be jealously preserved.

It is easy to understand the planning precepts that follow. Ancient city centers must be maintained as centers of economic functions and of social and cultural life: urban populations should cluster as closely around them as is possible on grounds of public health. When suburban sprawl threatens to weaken the links with the center, planning should seek to develop new town life around new town centers. Neighborhood ties are to be positively strengthened through physical planning arrangements; and since social mixture of different sorts and conditions of men is thought characteristic of the urban culture, the planning of neighborhoods should seek to ensure this too. Urban populations should have ready access to the countryside, whence come their supplies of foodstuffs, their recreation, their surviving link with the vital sense of nature; for this reason too, urban sprawl must be avoided.

European planners, working within a social system sympathetic to planning, have sought to realize these objectives in various ways; perhaps the best known are the new British towns, and the Swedish suburbs. In Britain, immediately after the Second World War, the government determined upon a vigorous policy of regional planning. So as to limit the further growth of London, new industrial location was to be controlled by an all-embracing system of licensing for new factories or extensions of existing ones. The physical spread of the London suburbs was to be stopped through the creation of a green belt, to be maintained in agriculture, recreation, and other fundamentally rural land uses, some five miles wide; outside this, a ring of new towns was to be created, combining new homes for Londoners displaced in renewal projects, with factory and other employment on the spot. These towns were to be built largely by state capital supplied to public development corporations, structured rather like the bodies that run Britain's nationalized industries. The factories were to be built by, or leased to, factory industry, which was to be diverted here through the operation of rigid industrial location controls on new factory development in the London area.

Remarkable as it may seem to an American audience, all the main lines of this policy have been retained by governments of varying political complexion (though, it must be said, with varying degrees of energy and enthusiasm) throughout the two decades since 1945. There are now eight new towns around London; they are thriving places with as many as 60,000 people. The industrialists have been so enthusiastic to establish factories there that the problem has now become rather to try and limit the growth there in the interests of development in other places. The rent rolls are even bringing considerable incomes back to the Development Corporations, and there is a general feeling that this is one of the more successful British examples of nationalized industry. At present, a whole series of even bigger new towns, and even new cities, are being planned in a further ring up to eighty miles around London; altogether, over thirty new towns and cities are in existence or at various stages of active planning in Britain, and by the last decade of this century they are certain to contain at least four million people.[1]

With smaller populations, smaller urban agglomerations and much more land relative to people, the Swedes clearly have a planning problem on a smaller scale than the British. Nevertheless, they have been equally concerned to control the growth of their biggest urban area, which at the present time has a total population (including unincorporated suburbs) of some 1.2 million people. Even in the first decade of this century, the Stockholm City Council was already taking the basic step to the control of the future growth of the city by buying, well in advance, virtually all the land that might be needed for future development all around. This has enabled them to ensure that all suburban development, whether by public authorities or private builders, has taken place according to master plans drawn up by the city. Since 1945 these plans have been based on a clear hierarchy of suburbs, each with local shopping and service centers, which are grouped together into a suburban unit of about 100,000 people. Though labeled suburbs, these areas are quite different from their contemporary American equivalents. In the first place, they are built at densities which are on average much higher, and which are pyramidical in form, reaching their highest levels near the center of each unit. In the second place, the centers are deliberately linked to a new, rail-based mass transit system, which links each group of suburbs with the next and with the metropolitan center. And thirdly, each unit in the group, and the group itself, is a physically distinct unit, separated from the others by planned open space.[2]

As with the English new towns, all this has been achieved only through a quite remarkable degree of governmental control, whether at the central or local level. And this, be it remembered, in democratic and relatively affluent societies—in the case of Sweden, indeed, affluent almost to North American levels. This acceptance of planning is essentially rooted in the more general upper middle class, whose traditional values the professional planners share with their peers in industry, commerce, and professional life generally. For, as the Italian historian, Benevolo, has shown, planning ceased to be in any sense a popular democratic movement after the failure of the 1848 revolutions in Europe; it was imposed by paternalist governments, whether these went under the name of Conservative, as in Bismarck's Germany, or of Social Democrat, as in Sweden or in Fabian England.[3] In this, it diverges profoundly from the pluralist, democratic basis of American society.

This is not to say that American planning is not heavily suffused with these same ideas. Indeed, a glance at any issue of the *Journal of the American Institute of Planners* would show that any decent professional American planner is committed, just as surely as his European counterpart, to the virtues of urbanity, rich urban centers, compact suburbs, green belts, and new town communities. In this sense, professional America and professional Europe share a common urban culture, which was born of long experience in Europe and transplanted to the cities of eastern North America long before the American Revolution. But the difference is that increasingly in North America these ideas have found themselves on alien soil. Webb, the historian of the Great Plains, showed how, on reaching the 98th meridian, farmers were forced to adapt their knowledge that had been derived from Europe.[4] Similarly, it can be argued that the nature of the city, inherited originally from Europe, altered profoundly in its passage across the continent, in a way that has never been fully appreciated. This transformation found its most complete expression where urban civilization flowered latest, in the far Southwest, in the mountain states, and in California: in metropolitan areas like Houston, Dallas, Phoenix, Las Vegas, and above all, Los Angeles. It constituted, in effect, a new culture, so different in degree from the old European urban culture that it became different in kind: I shall label it the *suburban culture.*

Essentially, unlike the old urban culture, this new phenomenon has found few intellectual defenders. After all, Las Vegas was effectively created by a gangster,[5] and most of the entrepreneurs and politicians who built up the new Western civilization, though doubtless respectable men, were too busy to be philosophical. And because American planners themselves were suffused with European notions about the good city, their reaction has been one of pure indignation.

In every department, form disintegrated: except in its heritage from the past, the city vanished as an embodiment of collective art and technics. And where, as in North America, the loss was not alleviated by the continued presence of great monuments from the past and persistent habits of social living, the result was a raw, dissolute environment and a narrow, constricted, and baffled social life.[6]

Sprawl is bad aesthetics; it is bad economics. Five acres are being made to do the work of one, and do it very poorly. This is bad for the farmers, it is bad for communities, it is bad for industry, it is bad for utilities, it is bad for the railroads, it is bad for the recreation groups, it is bad even for the developers.[7]

The question is, shall we have "slurbs," or shall we plan to have attractive communities which can grow in an orderly way while showing the utmost respect for the beauty and fertility of our landscape? If present trends continue, we shall have slurbs.[8]

The argument thus takes place on many fronts: the suburban form of development is attacked for wasting land, increasing commuter times, raising servicing costs, failing to preserve park land. But essentially the argument comes back to the *lack of form*. Mumford puts it best, in his appreciation of the ideas of regional development of the English garden city pioneer, Ebenezer Howard:[9]

A modern city, no less than a medieval town, . . . must have a definite size, form, boundary. It was no longer to be a mere sprawl of houses along an indeterminate avenue that moved towards infinity and ended suddenly in a swamp.

Here Mumford aligns himself specifically with the European tradition of urbanism. It is the same tradition which causes European visitors to puzzle over the apparent lack of form of the American urban landscape:[10]

Each building is treated in isolation, nothing binds it to the next one: there is a complete failure in relationship—odd, in a nation which has self-consciously exalted family relationship . . . to a new consciousness of "togetherness". . . . Yet togetherness in the landscape or townscape, like the coexistence of opposites, is essential.

Nairn gives to this characteristically formless, roadside civilization an expressive American word: "goop." Yet no one can deny that this civilization of the gas station and the hamburger bar—apparently endless, formless, sprawling, tasteless, exuberant—is the most characteristic single feature of the American landscape which I am trying to distinguish here, one without a real European imitator. This should suggest that what we witness in this controversy is not a simple battle

105

between the forces of mind and nonmind, civilization and anticiviliza-
tion; but rather a more fundamental and complex clash between two
modes of thinking and feeling: on the one hand, the European urban
culture transplanted to American soil; on the other, the specifically
American suburban culture that grew out from the earlier culture there.

I have said that this new culture has had few apologists. But the
rejection of the traditional city goes a long way back in American
intellectual life, at least to the time of the Revolution:[11]

> Jefferson did seriously influence the life of the nation with his talk of
> cancers on the body politic. . . . John Dewey's favorable view of pre-urban
> America has obviously had a great influence on the kind of education several
> generations of urban Americans have received.

More recently, and more specifically, there is the contribution of
Frank Lloyd Wright. Rightly, his biographer has written of Wright:[12]

> He was . . . a country boy who had spent all his life defending the simple
> hick-like things he had learned . . . against the condescension and scorn of
> urban sophisticates.

And Wright's great vision, Broadacre City, would have quite literally
earned the latter-day abusive epithet of prairie planning. For Wright's
criticism of the traditional European city is essentially the same as that
of a later generation of Californian planners:[13]

> No effective mobilization of the individual, making ten miles as one
> block nor any electrified means of human inter-communication then existed.
> Various physical contacts in that earlier day needed a certain congestion to
> facilitate and stimulate life. Life does not need them now in that way. . . .
> The new city will be nowhere, yet everywhere. Broadacre City.

Wright's vision specifically extends to a city based on the highway, in
which the regional shopping centers of postwar urban America were a
central feature:[14]

> Giant roads, themselves great architecture, pass public service stations
> now no longer eyesores but expanded as good architecture to include all

kinds of roadside service for the traveller . . . and imagine man-units so arranged and integrated each to the other that every citizen as he chooses may have all forms of production, distribution, self-improvement, enjoyment, within the radius of, say, ten to twenty miles of his own home. . . . This integrated distribution of living related to ground composes the great city that I see embracing this country. This would be the Broadacre City of tomorrow that is the nation. Democracy realised.

Here, then, finally is the older, preindustrial, pastoral vision of America, nurtured in the boyhood fields of Wisconsin and imaginatively transformed into what Banham has called the "posturban civilization" of Los Angeles.[15] The break with traditional urban culture is complete; the relationship to the "nonplace urban realm" of the modern Californian planners precise.

But it is to this Western American school of the 1960's that we look for the complete philosophical defense of the suburban culture:[16]

The Bay Area has become the region of the *new city* to a degree matched only in other parts of the Far West and exceeded perhaps only by Los Angeles. . . . It is fashionable, if extremely trite, to refer to the urban area as a shapeless sprawl, as a cancer, as an unrelieved evil. . . . The erroneous assumption that no such structure exists must result from a failure to study the dynamics of urban growth, or possibly from the desire to put forward a doctrine of what is "right" or "good" in urban growth.

Or, in the words of Robert B. Riley:[17]

The new city form has been damned simply because it is different. . . . The planning proposals made for these cities—and largely, too, for Eastern megalopolises—are based on nothing more or less than channeling growth back into a form that we recognise as the only true city—the traditional city. Such proposals are based on the unspoken assumption that a city is not really a city unless it has two attributes: high density and a centrist orientation.

The "new city" is marked by the fact that urban form has lost its old significance; it is no longer possible to allege that a particular set of urban functions and relationships has to be accommodated within a particular urban shape. This has profound consequences for planning. As Melvin Webber of Berkeley puts it:[18]

I contend that we have been searching for the wrong grail, that the values associated with the desired urban structure do not reside in the spatial structure per se. One pattern of settlement and its internal land use form is superior to another only as it better serves to accommodate ongoing social processes and to further the nonspatial ends of the political community. I am flatly rejecting the contention that there is an overriding universal spatial or physical aesthetic of urban form.

The fact, Webber argues, is that new systems of communication have exploded the centuries-old association between propinquity and communication. Only forty years ago the New York economist, Robert Murray Haig, published what is still the classic paper on urban location. In it he quoted the case of the New York architect who could reach anyone of importance in his business world in fifteen minutes from his office desk.[19] New York economists and planners are still prone to point to the advantages of agglomeration for certain sorts of businesses.[20] But, Webber argues, the automobile gives any establishment on Wilshire Boulevard as many linked establishments within a given time distance as does a similar establishment at Rockefeller Center. He says further:[21]

I would expect to find that Los Angeles residents maintain as diverse a range of contacts, that they interact with others as frequently and as intensively, that they are participants in as broad and as rich a range of communications as the resident of any other metropolitan area.

By decentralizing functions and providing for rapid and convenient access by freeway between them, Los Angeles can function effectively over a vast area, probably more effectively than the traditional centralized metropolis. Though in fact Los Angeles is a very dense city by the standards of the newer Western cities that have developed mainly since 1940, it had 5,200 persons per square mile in 1960, whereas Phoenix had only 2,400 per square mile.[22]

For the future, Webber forecasts a state where the constantly reducing real costs of transportation and communication will spread an urban culture freely across the face of the globe, limited only by the surviving need of some activities for proximity and by the fact that some locations are more attractive to live in and work in than others.

If Webber's analysis is right, in the not very distant future a form of urban—or more truly suburban—culture, on the Los Angeles model, could envelop virtually the whole world, all places will be easily accessible from almost all other places, and the *urban place* will be replaced by the *nonplace urban realm.*[23]

Webber's ideas are not completely new, as Broadacre City reminds us; they sit firmly in a Western American tradition. But as he has restated them, they represent the most radical and disturbing concept to enter the mainstream of planning thought for decades. If they are in any sense right, what we may be witnessing in Los Angeles is not the collapse of an honorable five-thousand-year-old urban tradition, but the birth of a totally new type of posturban culture. There is good reason to believe that California itself, in its social life and in its settlement forms, represents in pure essence tendencies that may take many years to influence fully the forms of eastern North America, perhaps decades to influence Europe. After all, it should never be forgotten that California had by 1925 reached the general living standards, and in particular the level of car ownership, of Europe in the late 1960's. It is possible, therefore, to regard the American Far West as a sort of vision of the entire Western world about the year 2000, modified only to the extent that different social and cultural traditions react to the patterns it offers. And this alone, in my submission, would justify examination of the challenge it seems to offer to our traditional views of urbanity.

It would be possible to do this from many different angles. But there are two in particular, which have been greatly illuminated by work in different disciplines—economic, sociological, geographic—in recent years. The first concerns the nature of suburban residential life, the value systems of the people who inhabit the new suburban subdivisions of the urban realm, their aspirations, the satisfaction of these aspirations, and the relation of all this to the planning of future suburbs. The other concerns the sphere of life which has traditionally been regarded as most specifically urban: the bundle of shopping functions, miscellaneous service functions, entertainment and culture, which has traditionally been gathered together in old city cores but which seems to be exploded into fragments in the new posturban system. Both these aspects are intimately concerned with what is, after all, the final aim of planning, subsuming efficiency and economics and good organization: simple human happiness and the chance to lead the good life. The central question we want to ask is whether we have evidence that the suburban culture represents an impoverishment of human life and human possibilities, in comparison with the old urban culture. We should not expect that the results of the research will provide any definite answers, at least answers that will satisfy dogmatists on either side. But since immediate and large decisions will depend on our provisional judgment, we should not defer it on that account.

THE QUALITY OF SUBURBAN SATISFACTIONS

Since 1950, particularly in North America, there has been a positive flood of sociological—and pseudosociological—work on the quality of life in the new suburbia. If one had to write a résumé of the essential conclusion of these works, it might read like this:

Up to a relatively late date—say, 1935—most urban Americans lived in incorporated cities, at fairly high densities. The high density, coupled with the great ethnic and social diversity of the city populations, made for a life rich in variety, contrast, and chance encounter. Many, especially the most recent generation of immigrants and their children, lived in extended families with a rich and complex network of kinship ties, which united the generations and provided a strong social cement that reduced the occurrence of delinquency and other forms of social malaise. Others, constituting the middle class, lived a life of great cultural freedom, with rich possibilities of choice in friends, entertainments, shopping, and life styles, all within easy reach. The new suburbia, in contrast, offers only homogeneity and conformity. Because population densities are low, the possibilities for fruitful human interaction are much reduced. Even the quality of material life, in the range of shopping goods and entertainments available, is impoverished and standardized. Because the new subdivisions are inhabited by people of the same age, education and social background, the awareness of different life styles and possibilities is atrophied. Because social relationships are restricted to the immediate neighborhood, there is a premium on conformity and a fear of the unusual and unknown. Because the population is transient, without roots, moving on always to the next rung in the status ladder, the society lacks the social cement that fixes standards, and readily tends to delinquency. Social relationships are shallow and are based almost wholly on the competitive acquisition of possessions. In such a soil, the growth of a really popular, democratic culture is stultified.

This, then, is the picture given by the mainstream of this recent sociological tradition. It is best summed up in quotations from two of the authors of classics in the genre—Riesman and Whyte:

There seems to me to be a tendency, though not a pronounced one, to lose in the suburbs the human differentiations which have made great cities in the past the centers of rapid intellectual and cultural advance. The suburb is like a fraternity house at a small college . . . in which likemindedness reverberates upon itself as the potentially various selves within each of us do not get evoked or recognized.[24]

People either learn as in California to drive great distances for dinner or confine themselves to their immediate environs. The central city as a meeting place disappears—a process which has gone further in Los Angeles and Chicago than in Boston or New York; the neighbors make up little circles based—as William H. Whyte, Jr., showed for Park Forest—largely on propinquity.[25]

The cities remain big enough for juveniles to form delinquent subcultures, but barely differentiated enough to support cultural and educational activities at a level appropriate to our abundant economy.[26]

In three important ways, I suggest, the city and the suburb represent antithetical values. They might be posed thus: mixture versus homogeneity; concentration versus dispersion; specialization versus the middle range.[27]

111

Since about 1960, this view has been subject to a great deal of critical sociological examination, which should have profoundly modified the intellectual view of suburbia. But, one suspects, it has not; indeed, since the later work confounds some popular intellectual shibboleths, it seems in some cases to have had a positively hostile reception—as witness the reviews in East coast newspapers of Herbert J. Gans' major study of *The Levittowners,* in summer 1967. In this section I wish to attempt a revaluation of the recent work.

A first critical point concerns the real nature of life in the old inner city—a life that a small and rapidly decreasing number of people can now accurately remember. The pioneer Chicago sociologist, Louis Wirth, as the author of a classic study of the ghetto, was in a better position than most to know, and he is commonly supposed to have given the definitive description of urban culture. Yet the account was in truth a highly critical one. According to him, urban populations could not hope to know each other properly, and "meet one another in highly segmented roles." He remarks on "the superficiality, the anonymity, and the transitory character of urban social relations." Close living and working together produced a competitive spirit that made for mutual exploitation. The "heightened mobility of the individual" reduced his sense of a binding tradition and as he was rarely a houseowner, he seldom achieved the capacity to be a neighbor.[28]

Yet, as Gans points out, Wirth's attempt to find universal urban characteristics really crudifies and blurs the issue. In truth, there are and always have been different urban subcultures. The culture that Wirth sought to describe was really that of the relatively restricted inner city, the zone of transition distinguished by the Chicago sociologists in their classic early work.[29] Indeed, it was on the basis of his work in the inner city that Robert Park distinguished the city as the place where indirect, "secondary" relations were substituted for the old direct, family or "primary" relations.[30] A variety of subcultures has to be distinguished. In some favored cities boasting a significant cosmopolitan upper middle class urban population (New York, San Francisco,

Boston, increasingly Washington) this group builds its own subculture. In addition, at least two other subcultures are clearly differentiated. The one is that described by Gans himself in the Italian West End of Boston, and by Young and Willmott in Bethnal Green in London, the urban village. According to Gans, "For most West Enders . . . life in the area resembled that found in the village or a small town, and even in the suburb."[31] This life was distinguished by a lack of relationship with the life of the wider city, except for its work places, and by an intense internal culture, based on the extended family—and, temporarily during adolescence for both sexes by extending into later life for the men, the peer group: "People do not, after marriage, throw off a past which contains their former family and friends. They combine past and present. They continue to belong to the same community."[32]

Thus, the urban village does not even have the character that Park and later Wirth ascribed to the city, or more properly to the inner city: it is essentially a subculture based on still surviving primary relationships. In contrast, however, Gans distinguishes another inner city subculture: the urban jungle.[33]

The second kind of area is populated largely by single men, pathological families, people in hiding from themselves or society, and individuals who provide the more disreputable of illegal-but-demanded services to the rest of the community. In such an area, life is comparatively more transient, depressed if not brutal, and it might be called an urban jungle.

This is a culture of secondary relationships, if any relationships at all. But it can more truly be labeled a pathological culture. Whereas the urban village is based on certain cultural beliefs like the primacy of family relationships, which is characteristic of the working class, here the values are those of the lower class: a culture based on the female-reared family and the marginal male. Such a culture, of course, is especially characteristic of part of the Negro populations that now occupy large parts of the urban jungle, although many Negro families share the working-class culture of the urban village.[34] The lower-class culture suffers from the basic problem that it can produce only unskilled workers, "men who find it increasingly difficult to survive in modern society, and who, in a more automated future, will be unable to do so."[35]

The inner city, in Gans' analysis, therefore consists of a number of relatively homogenous and separate groups. And many of these failed to exhibit the distinctive characteristics of inner city populations; indeed, the urban villagers in some important respects behave like suburbanites:[36]

That West Enders lived in five-story tenements and suburbanites occupy single-family houses made some—but not many—differences in their ways of life and the everyday routine. For example, although the West Enders were less than a mile from the downtown department stores, it is doubtful whether they used these more than the average suburbanite, who has to travel 45 minutes to get to them.

But this is to speak merely of a section of the inner urban population. When Gans came to consider the remainder of the urban population—a remainder that in most cases constitutes the great majority of the population within the city limits—he came to an even more surprising conclusion. Essentially, the way of life in these areas could be described as *quasi-primary*: though relationships between people were more guarded than in a true primary relationship, they were more intimate than in the story of secondary contact which Park thought characteristic of the city. But: "Postwar suburbia represents the most contemporary version of the quasi-primary way of life."[37] In other words, in this important respect no difference emerges between the outer residential areas of the incorporated city and the suburban neighborhoods. Other differences, too, prove illusory. Suburbs and outer city areas are both residential. The outer city areas are no nearer the central business district when time is taken as the measure, since transportation from the suburbs is usually faster. Many outer urban areas depend just as much on the automobile as do suburban ones. Though the outer urban areas are older and denser, they are likely to be just as socially homogeneous as the urban suburban areas; and this

114

is critical for social relationships. Therefore, Gans concludes, in its way of life the inner city has to be distinguished from the outer city and the suburbs, the latter two sharing a way of life little resembling traditional views of cities; even in the inner city, the life styles of many people bear little resemblance to the traditional picture; and physical and other differences between city and suburb are often spurious and without much meaning for ways of life.

There is added confirmation for this in Morris Janowitz's study of the local community newspapers of Chicago, to which David Riesman first drew attention. Janowitz could not find any clear association between readership of these papers and people's status, or their tendency to work or shop locally. What he did find was that these papers tended to be read by those who felt they had close links with the local community—those who thought it was really their home, who liked it, who saw it in terms of people rather than of physical attributes.[38]

These findings are not after all very remarkable. What distinguishes the outer urban areas and the suburbs from the inner city is that they are areas of middle-class families with children. These people have an intensely local, home-based life, though as Mowrer has pointed out, the husband as breadwinner will have another sphere of life at his factory or office:[39]

(In Chicago) the typical family unit in the new suburban areas consists of husband and wife with one or more children, with a tendency for those married couples who do not as yet have any children to live elsewhere than in the suburbs, or for those couples whose children have grown up to move either out of the suburbs, or to remain in the older sections. . . . About an equal proportion of newcomers have previously lived either in another suburb within the metropolitan area or in the central city and these constitute about four-fifths of all those who move in.

Thus the only difference between the suburb and the outer urban area may be that the latter is older and thus has an aging population. In the New York metropolitan area Hoover and Vernon found that the aging process in families, with the movement away of adult children, was a significant factor in the population decline of areas like the Bronx and Queens.[40]

The standard demographic pattern of suburbia obtained in the Long Island Levittown when Wattel studied it in the mid-1950's. Sixty-six per cent had come from New York City; the average adult in the community was 35 years old, and the household contained an average of a little over two children. And interestingly for the future of Levittown, it was a less mobile community than studies like Whyte's *Organization Man* would indicate. By 1956, more than half the population had lived in the community five or more years; one-quarter of the first (1947) arrivals had stayed, and one-fifth of the 1948 arrivals.[41]

These studies give a picture of communities that are homogeneous in terms of their age pattern and their family structure. And this, rather than any supposed social homogeneity or heterogeneity of the suburban population, really constitutes the central feature of suburban life. Nevertheless, the question of social mix has continued to obsess the sociologists and the planners. As Robert C. Weaver, Director of HUD, has baldly put it: "There can be, and there should be, an economic mix in the population of new communities in a democracy."[42]

Here, the detailed sociological investigations of Berger and Gans have been particularly important in throwing light on the true social nature of suburban society. Both researchers chose deliberately to study suburbs that were in no sense upper middle class: Berger's California suburb was specifically blue-collar; Gans' New Jersey Levittown was lower middle class. The results of these studies, I would suggest, must compel a profound reordering of our notions about suburbia.

Berger started by outlining the prevalent myth of the suburbs. This states that the suburban community is composed of transient, upwardly mobile, young, well-educated residents. It has a hyperactive social life based on voluntary organizations, in which the church is prominent. Its population is drawn from the city, and its breadwinners still go there to work. It is homogeneous in age, jobs, incomes, children, housing, furnishings, and tends to conformity and a very rigid "public" form of life.

Berger contrasted this mythical archetype with the actual pattern in his chosen Californian suburb. Here, the population spanned a wide income range. The population was so far from transient that 94 per cent thought their jobs were permanent, 73 per cent that they would stay in their present homes. Few had any expectation of upward social mobility. There was little participation in any form of social life: 70 per cent belonged to no clubs, organizations, or associations at all, and only 13 per cent said they visited their neighbors often. It is significant that 69.5 per cent of the two closest neighbors proved to be factory workers, and that nearly all the rest belonged to lower white-collar groups like bank tellers, postmen, and policemen.[43]

The fact, as Berger points out, is that most classic sociological studies of suburbs up to then had either been of upper-middle-class suburbs like Park Forest, Illinois,[44] or Forest Hill, Toronto,[45] or had alternatively emphasized the upper middle class characteristics of mixed or predominantly lower-middle-class communities.[46] It may well be that the suburbs of New York, Chicago and Toronto took on predominantly upper-middle-class characteristics, which had been developed earlier in their growth. But it seems certain that in the future many, if not most, suburbs will be occupied by lower middle or working class, with very different life styles:[47]

> There are good reasons for believing that "organization" men live as Whyte says they do, and that the "new" middle class lives as others say they do. But there is no reason to believe that what is characteristic of "organization" men or of the "new" middle class is also characteristic of the mass-produced suburbs . . . references to "suburbia" more often than not cite the examples of Park Forest and Levittown—as if these two communities could represent a nation-wide phenomenon that has occurred at all but the lowest income levels and among most occupational strata.

The interesting result of this intellectual bias is almost certainly a complete misinterpretation of the nature of mass suburbia. Upper-middle-class suburbs like Park Forest are supposed to be the seats of aggressive upward social mobility; but Berger shows that his working-class families neither are more middle class nor feel more middle class than before. Therefore the paradox is that the intellectuals are attacking working-class suburbanites for cultural traits of which they are completely innocent:[48]

> By accepting the myth of suburbia, the liberal and left-wing critics are placed in the ideologically weak position of haranguing the suburbanites precisely for the meaninglessness they attribute to the very criteria of their success. The critic . . . warns: "You may think you're happy, you smug and prosperous striver, but I tell you that the anxieties of status mobility are too much."

It is however Gans' analysis of Levittown, New Jersey, which has provided final inversion of the suburban myth. In Gans' words:[49]

> The findings on changes and their sources suggest that the distinction between urban and suburban ways of living postulated by the critics (and by some sociologists as well) is more imaginary than real. Few changes can be traced to the suburban qualities of Levittown, and the sources that did cause change, like the house, the population mix, and newness, are not distinctively suburban. Moreover . . . when suburbs are compared to the large urban residential areas beyond the downtown and inner districts, culture and social structure are virtually the same among people of similar age and class. Young lower middle class families in these areas live much like their peers in the suburbs, but quite unlike older, upper middle class ones, in either urban or suburban neighborhoods.

As Gans points out, many of the changes that did occur were desired before the move; because the move makes them possible, people feel more satisfied with life than before, chiefly through a more intensive family life. Some changes do occur under the pressure of suburban life: a greater degree of community organization, for instance. But these changes affect different people in different ways and to different degrees. And the fact is that, according to Gans, the suburbanites refuse to fit most of the labels that earlier sociologists had tried, implicitly or explicitly, to pin on them:[50]

Levittowners are not really members of the national society, or for that matter, of a mass society. They are not apathetic conformists ripe for takeover by a totalitarian elite or corporate merchandiser; they are not conspicuous consumers and slaves to sudden whims of cultural and political fashion, they are not even organization men or particularly other-directed personalities. . . . Their culture may be less subtle and sophisticated than that of the intellectual, their family life less healthy than that advocated by psychiatrists, and their politics less thoughtful and democratic than the political philosophers' —yet all of these are superior to what prevailed among the working and lower middle classes of past generations.

For the future, Gans sees suburbs having some positive consequences for the next generation of young parents, as his studies show they have had for this generation. At least some forms of class division should weaken as the boundaries between middle class, lower middle class and working class get progressively blurred. Though much building will still take place in small subdivisions, there may be more large developments of the Levittown type; and these should guarantee a greater degree of variety in the suburban scene.

But the influence of suburbia on social mores is not an account to be exaggerated. The central contribution of Berger and Gans to our understanding of suburban sociology is precisely this: that the physical form of development has only a very limited effect on life styles, and is to be seen rather as a reflection of what people wanted before the development ever took place. Sociology up to that time had considered extraordinary people in suburbia and had emerged in consequence with a quite distorted picture of a new pattern of suburban civilization. Berger and Gans looked at ordinary people in suburbia, and concluded that these people would be living in much the same way, with much the same pattern of social relationships, whether they lived in areas called urban or areas called suburban. According to Gans:[51]

The planner has only limited influence over social relationships. Although the site planner can create propinquity, he can only determine which houses are to be adjacent. He can thus affect visual contacts and initial social contacts among their occupants, but he cannot determine the intensity or quality of the relationships. This depends on the characteristics of the people involved.

True, the character of the residents—their social homogeneity, or otherwise—can be affected by planning the homogeneity or otherwise of the dwellings they will occupy. But in practice, this is controlled much more by developers and by financiers, and in the last resort by the operation of the market, than by the decision of the planners. In a society where houses are built to be sold, this could hardly be otherwise. Gans' own conclusion, which seems to me reasonable, is that the planner cannot and should not prescribe any ideal pattern of social life; he should merely see that the opportunity for maximum choice is given, for instance, in the vital matter of remaining within the family circle or becoming gregarious. Similarly, the planner can provide for a certain heterogeneity of race and class and religion, which again allows choice in social relationships, but always provided that within local blocks there is enough homogeneity to ensure lack of conflict and a sense of common values.

Above all, Gans argues, the planner in suburbia must beware of trying to impose his own value system on people with quite different value systems, which he simply cannot appreciate:[52]

> If he considers traffic congestion or a long commuting trip undesirable, but the commuters do not, he must provide evidence for his proposals. . . . But if there are no serious negative consequences to a long jouney to work, the planner cannot expect people to make sacrifices just because he thinks a shorter journey would be good for them.

This particularly applies to what is probably the greatest common fetish of planners, the world over: the search for higher suburban densities. These are advocated for all sorts of reasons: to save land, cut sprawl, shorten commuting times, reduce monotony, and increase urbanity. But: "Few actual or potential suburbanites share these attitudes, because they do not accept the business efficiency concept and the upper middle class, anti-suburban esthetic built into them."[53]

This conclusion, I would suggest, has very large implications. By and large, it is fair to say that planners have been antisuburban; if they have lived with suburbia, have even helped to design it, they have tried essentially to modify it, to turn it into their own vision of urbanity. Gans is now arguing that the values of the planners are themselves in large measure not professional values, but are class values deriving from the society in which the planners live. In a real sense, they are antidemocratic, unless it can be shown that suburbia has antisocial consequences that have not been foreseen by those who build it, and the case here does not seem to have been made.

SUBURBAN CENTERS AND THE METROPOLITAN HIERARCHY

In the last section, we have looked principally at suburbia, so to speak, from the residential end: we have considered that sphere of life which ends at people's front doors. But even if we accept Gans' conclusion that the planner should not try to create social forms by order, there do remain important planning problems of social relationships in suburbia. For people must come together in suburbia: their cars are driven on the same highways, their children are educated at the same schools, they do their shopping and they seek their services in common centers. In this section I want to look more closely at this communal aspect of life, with particular reference to the planning of retail and service centers in suburbia.

Here, too, is an area rich in planning myth. Reduced to its common elements, the myth says, approximately: the downtown area of the central American city is in a state of collapse. This is the result of inability to accommodate the motor car, coupled with the dispersion of the population into suburbs and the decay of the inner city areas immediately surrounding downtown. As this has apparently been an inevitable and irreversible price in all American cities, we can expect that European cities will follow suit as the process of suburbanization gains momentum. Within the suburbs, shopping is concentrated in large regional shopping centers based on very large supermarkets, in which all the emphasis is on standardization of product, with a consequent lack of the variety and choice which was a feature of the old downtown. Most serious of all, the new centers are planned from the start as single-land-use, retailing islands surrounded by superhighways. When the supermarkets shut their doors, they are deserted within minutes. The suburbs therefore totally lack what the old city possessed in abundance: the rich, varied life made possible by the mixture of land uses and in particular by the presence of a dense residential population in the inner city.

It seems to be important to examine closely this myth, to decide which elements of it are true and which not, and to judge then how important a problem remains. Is it finally true that suburbia lacks the great urban centers that distinguished the old European civilization, and if so, how important is this for the quality of life? Even if Gans is right in arguing that the planner should restrict himself to providing better choice for suburbanites, does this demand that he create the possibility of urban styles of life if these are proved to be lacking? Or is this, once again, an area where the planner is trying to impose his own class-based value system on people with completely different values?

Perhaps it is most helpful to look first at the facts. In the last decade, extensive work by geographers has established very clearly the basic pattern of retail and service centers which is developing in the suburbs of North American metropolitan areas. Indeed, it is now possible to speak of a general model of metropolitan area centers, within which one can more clearly perceive the dynamic changes that take place over time.

The first feature of this model, paradoxically, is the continuing dominance of downtown. None of the research in the last decade has yet seriously shaken the conclusion of Jonassen in 1955, based on a study of shoppers' attitudes in three North American cities:[54]

In the opinion of the majority, the central business district has decided advantages, offering better services, better quality and cheaper prices. The downtown area may retain these advantages because it has a greater number of actual and potential customers than are available elsewhere.

Even then, changes were taking place, with a greater and greater proportion of trade passing to the suburban centers. The effect was a redistribution of functions; downtown facilities would increasingly serve more specialized requirements, whereas more frequent and common needs would increasingly be met in suburban centers. At the same time, a growing suburban population would allow the suburban centers to provide a wider range of goods; but rising incomes would mean that people's appetite for specialized products would increase more than proportionately, so that the advantages of downtown for this type of shopping would remain. Futhermore, Jonassen pointed out, the very infrequency of these specialized demands made the parking difficulties in the downtown area less important than they would seem at first sight.[55]

These conclusions were reached before the arrival of the very big regional shopping center, serving 100,000 and more people, in the suburbs; for such centers only began to be developed on any scale in the late 1950's and early 1960's. Yet in the San Francisco Bay Area, where the process went as far and as fast as anywhere on the North American continent, James E. Vance could still repeat in 1962 the same conclusions as Jonassen seven years earlier. The new suburban centers proved to have not merely a minimum but also a maximum population, set by the possibility of competition from other centers. This meant that their ability to provide a wide range of specialized goods was severely limited. Two-thirds of the customers in these centers came from a tributary area extending only 4.5-5.5 miles from the center. Increasingly, therefore, a division of functions was emerging in the Bay Area: there were centers providing a restricted range of standardized goods for a geographically limited suburban market, on the one hand, and on the other a metropolitan core area, providing specialized goods and services for the entire metropolitan market. Within this framework, it was true that in statistical terms the core was relatively losing trade to the suburban centers. But this was in part a mere statistical effect: the suburban centers were increasing their trade rapidly because of the demands of increasing suburban populations for convenience goods, whereas the core was increasing its trade much more slowly. The overall statistical trend concealed what was the most important change—a profound re-sorting of the character of the trade:[56]

> The emerging pattern of commercial geography in the United States is the separation of mass selling from speciality selling with the removal of the former from the central business district save for that part which serves the local population within the central city.

The most meticulously documented study of commercial structure yet in an American city, that of Berry and his colleagues in Chicago, comes to a strikingly similar conclusion to Vance's work:[57]

> Much has been written recently about the decline of the central business district. The consensus of research findings, however, now appears to be that the decline is largely percentagewise rather than absolute, a trick of statistics as suburbs grow and are provided with local shopping facilities. . . . Most central business districts, Chicago's among them, appear to have remained largely at an aggregate equilibrium over the past decade, no longer expanding because they are reaching as far as they can.

In fact, the Chicago central business district in 1958 accounted for 14.6 per cent of all retail sales and 31.06 per cent of all shopping (comparison) goods sales, on only 0.5 per cent of the ground area of the city. It sold ten times as much as the largest outlying center. According to Berry:[58]

> But size is not the only criterion for setting apart the CBD. . . . The CBD provides a greater range of shoppers' goods than the outlying centers, and sells them not only to the entire city and metropolitan area, but to the midwestern United States, and for a few things, to the United States as a whole.

This conclusion is a comforting one for retailers in the central business districts of American cities. But against it there stands the conclusion of the researchers Meyer, Kain, and Wohl in their meticulously detailed study, *The Urban Transportation Problem:*[59]

In no instance is there any evidence of sharp increase in CBD employment. Similarly, there is every indication that the number of downtown shoppers has declined as well. Overall, the evidence points to . . . frequent instances of stagnation, and only a few instances of moderate growth in central-city activity.

In fact, Meyer, Kain, and Wohl's statistical evidence is somewhat ambiguous and inconclusive on the critical point of central shopping patterns. They show that overall, in 39 large standard metropolitan statistical areas, CBDs experienced an 0.1 per cent gain per annum in sales during 1948-1958, and only a marginal 0.3 per cent loss in the more recent period 1954-1958. As they point out, only the 13 fastest growing SMSAs actually recorded increase in CBD sales in either period (amounting to as much as 0.6 per cent per annum during 1948-1958); the rest experienced losses. But again these were not dramatic: for medium-growing SMSAs they were 0.1 per cent per year during 1948-1958 and for slow growing SMSAs also 0.1 per cent per year.[60] Overall, the conclusion still stands: downtown is stagnating in retail sales, while suburban sales increase owing to the demands of expanding suburban population.

In this changing situation, specialization is the strength of the central core. And as Vance argues for the Bay Area, offices will remain there too; indeed, they will increasingly dominate them. Because the office district commonly depends (at least in part) on mass transportation whereas the specialty shops depend on the car-based customer, the optimal location for the two is likely to diverge quite markedly; so that the future central business district may consist of two clearly defined modes, the office center and the specialized shopping (or boutique) center. There are clear signs of this segregation developing in some rapidly growing North American cities today: Toronto is a specially good example.

Working quite separately in Europe, the Swedish economist Folke Kristensson has reached similar conclusions. According to him, there is an important and rapidly growing complex of functions that will continue to want to be in central cores; it includes central decision

125

making, intelligence, investigations, negotiations, and publicity, converging into formulations on strategic and tactical matters. Other groups—routine information handling and specialized, technically complex production—will remove from the center under market pressures, but will probably prefer to relocate nearby. In Stockholm, Kristensson has recommended the creation of a special area for these functions in a zone west of the city center. According to Kristensson's calculations for Stockholm, 20 per cent of all metropolitan employment will continue to be in the core: this includes not merely the office functions, but specialized shopping and services. Another 25 per cent will need to be in the zone adjacent to the center; allowing 15 per cent of employment to be migratory in nature, this leaves fully 40 per cent of employment to be placed in suburban locations.[61] It can readily be seen that in a fast-growing metropolitan area, this could actually spell an increasing amount of employment in the central core, rather than the reverse.

In the suburbs themselves, the studies of the geographers reveal a very clear hierarchy of centers. The lowest, most local center is the neighborhood center. According to different studies it caters to between 1,500 and 20,000 people; but for new shopping centers planned today, between 7,500 and 15,000 people is probably the minimum that could be considered.[62] Such centers, in Voorhees' calculations, had on average about 41,000 square feet of shopping floor space. The biggest tenant would usually be a supermarket; other occupants would include a drug store, dry cleaner, service station, and barber and beauty shops. The middle range is supplied by the community center, based on a population of between 15,000 and 30,000 people and with a shopping area of as much as 150,000 square feet; here, the main store would be a variety store of the 5-and 10-cent variety, or a junior department store. Lastly, and most importantly, came the regional center, serving 100,000 and more people, and with an average floor space area of 410,000 square feet. There is general agreement among researchers that these centers will be built around at least one full department store and that they will offer a full range of standard shopping (comparison) goods.[63]

Two points about this hierarchy are exceptionally important for the future of the suburbs. The first concerns the present maximum size of regional center; the second, the dynamics of future change. In 1956, Kelley could report that different workers quoted tributary populations for regional centers which ranged from 50,000 to as much as 100,000 to one million.[64] More recently, Berry and his colleagues have calculated that in Chicago the major unplanned regional centers serve areas which average 300,000 people (ranging from 5 to 20 square miles) for shopping goods, but only 65,000 (averaging 2.5 square miles) for convenience goods.[65] Almost simultaneously, Vance has shown that in the Bay Area the eleven major regional centers have an average of 237,000 people within five miles, but with a very wide range.[66] His conclusion was that this size of tributary population was likely to remain restricted by the ability of competing centers to draw off the trade in standardized goods, by virtue of the critical importance of convenience for this type of shopping. Therefore, there seems to be some agreement here that even the largest regional shopping centers, in a metropolitan area with normal modern North American densities and distributions of population, cannot hope to command tributary populations of much more than 250,000-300,000 population. Many centers may well function effectively with less.

This conclusion compares with the experience of Sweden, which is particularly interesting because it demonstrates the pattern that emerges with very high per capita incomes but with acceptance of rigid city planning norms in a way that is quite foreign to North America. Here, in the City of Stockholm the metropolitan area plans of the late 1940's and early 1950's were based on new suburbs built around a very similar hierarchy of neighborhood ("D") centers, community ("C") centers, and regional ("B") centers, with possible provision for future superregional ("A") centers. At first the hierarchy was based on very small catchment populations, as little as 3,000-6,000 for the "C" centers and 10,000 for the "B" centers. But experience in the 1950's and early 1960's taught that people were willing to move farther to shop, in order to find a wider range of goods, than was originally thought. The "C" centers are now based on populations of about 10,000-15,000, mainly for convenience goods, and the "B" centers for populations of between 50,000 and 100,000, which appears low by North American standards but which permits the development of downtown department store branches. Lately there have been signs of demand for a still more steeply peaked hierarchy, and Stockholm regional planners are talking of a possible two-level system with nothing between the local neighborhood group of shops and the major regional center.[67]

This last point relates to another; the dynamics of shopping demand. It is reasonable to suppose that on the whole, suburban populations in North America and Western Europe will become more mobile rather than less. Additionally, as income levels rise the demands for a wide range of specialized goods may confidently be expected to rise also. Nor does this merely affect the demand for what are conventionally called "comparison" or "shopping" goods. To take an instance: as the sales of cookbooks rise, and as more and more housewives take to more adventurous recipes, the range of specialized and even exotic goods to be carried in the supermarkets will rise accordingly. It may well be indeed that the supermarkets will not be well equipped to deal with this type of demand and that an increasing need may be felt for the specialized delicatessen. All this is likely to raise somewhat the optimal size of the catchment area of the regional suburban centers. But especially in view of Vance's findings in the Bay Area, this trend should not be exaggerated. The best description of the likely process is still probably that of Garrison, in 1959:[68]

The nucleated system of shopping centers will be subject to even greater concentration, smaller shopping centers will lose functions which can be provided more efficiently by larger centers but, in turn, will gain functions from still smaller shopping centers. It is moot as to the exact location system which will evolve. . . . A transportation system with the facilities oriented in terms of present land uses will tend to maintain the present location structure of shopping centers. A transportation system oriented in terms of presumably desirable reorientations of population and centers will lead to some other location stucture.

Garrison's conclusion is particularly important when comparing North American experience with European. For nearly all of Europe has a centuries-old tradition of urbanism in a way that much of North America has not, and this fact alone is bound to affect the dynamics of the central place system within a growing metropolitan area. As Dutch geographer Wissink put it, in the course of an extended study of European and American suburbanization:[69]

In general, cities with a long history are apt to have a structure that differs considerably from that of young cities. Not only do they show a considerable degree of structural maturity, but they also contain vestiges of their past in physical build and structure, which continue to be of great influence on present development. . . . Former old villages and towns, which have nearly or completely been absorbed by the European city, often have retained a much more vigorous life of their own than in and around American cities, thus contributing considerably to a variety district by district.

The fact is likely to be of great importance in very large, fast-growing metropolitan areas. As the German economist Lösch first notes, important metropolitan centers tend somewhat to inhibit the development of rival centers within the near vicinity. Nevertheless, lower order centers will develop, in the form of market towns, in certain sectors radiating out from the city which are rich in transportation routes.[70] As suburbanization proceeds, it is likely to take place most rapidly in these sectors, since they provide a higher level of accessibility with the center of metropolitan area. Thereupon, the local demands of the suburban population for convenience goods are likely to focus upon these market centers, unless planners take very firm action to provide new centers. But the politics of local planning are such that they cannot ordinarily do this, quite apart from the fact that their basic prejudices are in favor of concentrating shopping in centers that look and feel "urban" in character.

129

The result, which is very clearly seen in the area forty miles around London, is a positive explosion of shopping within the former market towns. The old small shops are increasingly taken over by big national chains, dealing in convenience goods (food) and standardized shopping goods (for instance ready-made clothing). There is normally an extension of the shopping area through a redevelopment of old, outworn property on one or more sides of the former central district of the town. Since car ownership levels are high, in some areas approaching North American levels, the resulting problems of traffic congestion and car parking become acute. They are alleviated in part by new inner ring roads and the provision of publicly or privately owned off-street parking; this often involves considerable amounts of subsidy either from local taxation sources or even, in the case of highway construction, from central government funds. The process, which in the London region has only been partially modified by the building of eight new towns and their associated shopping centers, has taken place almost piecemeal and unrealized, as a product of the great and unexpected growth of population since the Second World War. Its result has been that the old centers have greatly increased their role as central places within the metropolitan hierarchical system.[71] It has been argued with justice that its effect has been to impose a very heavy burden of the social costs of redevelopment on the community as a whole, through subsidies and associated taxation, compared with the alternative of developing completely new suburban shopping centers.[72]

Such centers could have taken a North American form, being planned by private developers as segregated shopping developments not normally associated with other land uses. Despite the rising levels of car ownership in Western Europe since 1955, this has been a model followed in only a very few places, such as the Main-Taunus center near Wiesbaden and the Ruhrpark near Bochum, both in Western Germany. Apparently these two developments have been commercially successful but there is not much sign in 1967 of their being followed on a wide scale. Otherwise isolated attempts at developing out-of-town centers, mainly through American finance—such as the GEM center at West Bridgford near Nottingham, in England—have not been a conspicuous commercial success. The financial results of the first English Woolco one-stop shopping center, which opened in 1967 at Oadby near Leicester, are being awaited with a great deal of interest in the British retailing world.

The biggest European developments in suburban shopping, in fact, have been a radically different form. They have been planned and built by municipalities or public corporations as part of fully planned new suburbs or new towns, and then leased to private owners. The most notable examples are the shopping centers of the eight new towns in the ring 20-35 miles out of London, and the regional "B" centers of the Stockholm suburbs which have already been described. Significantly, both were planned initially to serve the needs of local populations arriving principally on foot or by public transport, with only a very modest provision for car parking. But since the plans allowed sufficient flexibility for extra parking, they have attracted motorized shoppers from a wider radius. In Stockholm, for instance, the first "B" center at Vällingby (1954) provided initially for only 650 parked cars; since then, space for another 600 has been provided. The second "B" center at Farsta (1960) provided for 2,250 parked cars from the start.[73] Despite this, an important part of the trade of the Stockholm "B" centers comes from the areas of higher density apartment housing within walking distance of the shops, which contain between 20,000 and 25,000 people. This contrasts sharply with the experience in the American regional centers, some of which are virtually inaccessible save by car.

THE NONPLACE SUBURBAN REALM

The study of the metropolitan central place system, then, seems merely to demonstrate that the same statistical set of facilities can be provided and is being provided in very different physical ways, depending on history and popular social habits and preferences of planners. Certain features of the suburban myth do prove, apparently, to be true: thus suburbs will develop centers providing a wide range of standardized goods but very little of the variety we associate with great urban centers, and these centers will not possess the varied land use of old centers. Certain other features appear to be as categorically untrue; the big urban center continues to dominate the metropolitan hierarchy and may even gain added strength and vitality from specialization, while the suburban centers themselves can be entirely separated from the suburbs they serve or are integrated closely into the suburbs themselves. The question is, do the differences matter? Is the preservation of the historic city center a matter for any concern? Should planners try to provide as much richness and variety of experience as possible within the new suburban centers, even if they cannot hope to emulate the old urban ones?

This, finally, appears to be the point where European planning wisdom (and with it, conventional or East Coast American planning wisdom) separates from the new Californian school of planning. Webber's and Vance's Californian "nonplace urban realm" is essentially a *suburban* realm, dominated by a free movement along freeways to centers that allow one to buy goods, to obtain services, to make contacts with people, in physical circumstances that bear almost no relationship to the old European notions of urban living. The Californian planners would emphatically deny that this pattern of life is in any significant way less rich, less varied, than the way of life lived in the old traditional city. The East Coast planners, represented most forcibly by Jane Jacobs,[74] would find almost no common ground with them.

In all this, there has been a good deal of subjective prejudice but few facts. Recently, though, some important research has been done in Europe on popular attitudes to city life, most notably in Holland. In Amsterdam, a city with a particularly historic and rich urban core, a sample of 320 people were asked both about their attitudes to the core, and about their actual use of it. Of the 320, 63 were classed as "enjoyers" (that is, they both used and enjoyed the historic core), whereas another 131 were classed as "sympathizers" (that is, they liked

132

the core but did not use it much). Therefore, some two-thirds of those asked had a highly positive attitude to the core.[75] But it is to be noted that in the attractiveness of its central core Amsterdam is almost certainly unique in the Netherlands. The Dutch Institute for Public Opinion Research has asked for people's judgment as to the city with best quality of public life and entertainment. Unsurprisingly, Amsterdam scored over 40, whereas no other city in the country scored more than 10. Significantly, 43 per cent of the nation-wide sample had visited the city in the previous year, including 87 per cent of the residents in the city outside the core and 42 per cent of those living within 25 miles.[76]

The attractive quality of the Amsterdam urban core, it appears, is closely bound up with a highly concentrated and highly specialized resident population; single persons, especially unmarried young women, young families with no children, artists, students, scientific workers, journalists, workers in restaurants, and foreigners—"In general, a rather heterogeneous and shifting, but vital and lively population."[77] Similarly, detailed work does not seem to exist on the demographic structure of other Dutch cities. But it appears more than likely that in its population characteristics, Amsterdam is unique; and that the demands stemming from this population provide a good deal of its unique character. In other words, the urban quality of Amsterdam is not something that can be widely emulated.

The groups who dominate the urban core of Amsterdam in fact, are the same groups listed in America by William H. Whyte as the people most likely to continue supporting an urban civilization in America—the people engaged in the communications industry, the transients, the academics, the young unmarrieds, and the childless couples. They form, Whyte suggested, a disproportionately large part of the housing market of the inner city.[78] But statistically each kind represents only a small fraction of total American households, and the critical question is precisely how many urban centers they could occupy at a density sufficient to affect the character of urban life. As Paul H. Ylvisacker has put it:[79]

Manhattan will survive longer than most; an exception, but a changing and misleading one. . . . It is not a model for the core cities of our 200 metropolitan areas; it is more a rival, siphoning off much of the economic and social potential of the Philadelphias, the Bostons, and even the Chicagos. It is sustained by those very forces which are contributing to urban dispersion throughout the country.

Or in the words of John Burchard:[80]

Big cities are bound to pose some disadvantages and many people find the prices too high. For most of them the answer probably is that they really do not care much about variety of choice and have no unusual yearnings.

This is almost identical with the conclusion of Herbert Gans:[81]

Some young people may be persuaded to remain in or return to the city by urban renewal programs, but their numbers are not likely to be large, for even with increasing college attendance, the proportion of city-loving cosmopolitans remains minute.

The conclusion from North America, then, appears depressingly unanimous. Urban culture has become a minority culture, practiced only by upper-middle-class cosmopolitans in isolated islands. Within the North American continent Manhattan appears to form one such island and San Francisco (probably on account of its geographical isolation) another. View it how you will, the invasion of San Francisco's Haight-Ashbury district by some 50,000 "hippies," during the summer of 1967, was one of the more remarkable mass colonizations in modern American urban history; but the "hippies" themselves, like the beat generation of the 1950's and the hobos of the 1920's, belong to an old tradition of restlessness, of dissociation from conventional values, which is almost as old as America itself.

Such movements may grow; whatever form they take from year to year, the growth of affluence and restlessness among the young may well mean that bigger groups of transients invade the cities, at least for short periods. Yet they are still unlikely to represent more than a minority culture. This is not, however, to say that there will not be many centers of focus, of gathering, of specifically urban excitement within the new suburban culture. The mistake of traditional planners may indeed be precisely this: in their anxiety to keep centers of liveliness, of attractiveness, they confused this function with a traditional physical form (the close-knit European inner city) and a traditional way of life (the small-scale, face-to-face, cosmopolitan culture of the old city). The new nonplace suburban realm can manage its gathering points too; but they may bear little resemblance to planners' traditional dreams. I think of Tom Wolfe's account of Las Vegas:[82]

> One can see the magnitude of the achievement. Las Vegas takes what in other American towns is but a quixotic inflammation of the senses for some poor salary mule in the brief interval between the flagstone rambler and the automatic elevator downtown and magnifies it, foliates it, embellishes it into an institution. For example, Las Vegas is the only town in the world whose skyline is made up neither of buildings, like New York, nor of trees, like Wilbraham, Massachusetts, but signs. One can look at Las Vegas from a mile away on Route 91 and see no buildings, no trees, only signs. But such signs! They tower, they revolve, they oscillate, they soar in shapes before which the existing vocabulary of art is helpless.

The Strip in Las Vegas is a six-mile line of hotels and casinos, set in the middle of an uninhabitable desert. It has been created, essentially, in its entirety since 1946. Its architecture of signs, as Wolfe says, gives it a quality it shares with Versailles: it is one of the few architecturally uniform cities in the history of Western civilization. And this is surely no accident, for these are two cities created purely as the pleasure places of an affluent class. Now Las Vegas has nothing whatsoever to do with anything that any self-respecting planner would call urban; yet in its exhilarating display of unself-conscious pop art, it is one of the most essentially urban places in the world. To my knowledge, only the English architectural critic, Reyner Banham, has yet had the precipience to notice this.[83] The same verdict goes, I think, for Sunset Strip, in Los Angeles, or any of the blazing technicolor thoroughfares of America's new West coast civilization. It even goes, on a more modest scale, for any of the motel-and-burger-joint strips that run along the main radial highways for miles outside any sizable American city.

135

These developments are the purest anathema to any self-respecting planner of the traditional school of European urbanism. It is not difficult to see why. In the traditional planning canon, urban excitement is necessarily based on small-scale, face-to-face contact and a high density of people interacting on the ground. Vehicles are a distraction and if possible should be banned; this is why boulevards are stigmatized as bad environmental planning, even where (as in Berlin's Kurfürstendamm) they are demonstrably successful in attracting crowds. And development on a scale that accepts the motor vehicle, and that is meant to be appreciated by a motorized crowd rather than a pedestrian crowd, is ipso facto bad. Yet this is precisely the point of Fremont Street or Sunset Strip, or the whole of Wilshire or La Cienega Boulevard in Los Angeles. And any attempt to judge Los Angeles on the same scale as traditional cities is a mistake. Kevin Lynch made this mistake in looking at what is conventionally still called the central area of Los Angeles, but what is in fact the zone of discard behind the explosion of the real central area along a fifteen-mile strip, westwards to the sea. Yet the people he interviewed gave him a clear sense of this different scale. He writes:[84]

But there was some evidence that orientation at the regional scale was not too difficult. . . . Below this grand scale, however, structure and identity seemed to be quite difficult. . . . Automobile traffic and the highway system were dominant themes in the interviews. This was the daily experience, the daily battle—sometimes exciting, usually tense and exhausting. There were frequent references to the overpasses, the fun of the big interchanges, the kinesthetic sensations of dropping, turning, climbing. For some persons, driving was a challenging, high speed game.

There is, I think, a point of critical importance which emerges from these replies: a point Lynch himself seized, when he put forward his schematic suggestion for a decentralized, multinuclear metropolis.[85] It is that people en masse, ordinary people, can adapt themselves—not without strain, to be sure, but certainly not without excitement and exhilaration, too—to the new scale and the new technological demands of the Californian supercity. Its importance lies in the very fact that in some critical ways, Los Angeles is the metropolis that represents all our futures: a vision of twenty-first-century urbanization, so to speak, already available to us in the twentieth. One might apply to it the comment which one observer once applied, with much less justice, to the Soviet Union: I have seen the future, and it works.

Left to themselves, the forces of the market could produce such a new style of urban landscape in Europe too. And in countries with more permissive planning systems, such as Belgium or Italy, there are pale imitations, but they lack the confidence and panache of their American originals. The scale of urban development is steadily growing, inexorably, under pressure of economic and social forces: super-city already exists, in southeast England and in the Dutch Randstad and in the Rhine-Ruhr region of Western Germany, as surely as in California. Yet within the new structure, the old urban places retain their primacy, not only in economic terms, but as foci of urban excitement. And where the accidents of history have created small nation states, like Belgium or the Netherlands, there is evidence that even these can support a flourishing metropolis apiece. One can argue even that by dividing a nation state into a number of semiautonomous provinces, as in Federal Germany after World War II, it is possible to obtain a form of metropolitan culture in a number of separate provincial cities. There is certainly a sensible difference between the quality of life in Munich, Stuttgart, or Hamburg and that in major French provincial cities of the order of Lyon, Bordeaux, or Strasbourg.

THE FUTURE METROPOLIS

This paper has ranged long and wide. It has aimed to gather together the implications of recent research and speculation about the future of metropolitan areas in two continents. The evidence seems to point to certain conclusions, which I want to emphasize.

First, it is clear that there is a powerful and long-standing trend in all advanced industrial countries towards a progressive suburbanization of the population. It would be interesting, and to some, refreshing, if I could report new and startling evidence that this process was occurring against people's wills and was about to be reversed by popular acclaim; but for this there is absolutely no evidence that I know of. On the contrary: the sociological surveys from North America indicate that the great mass of the population, who belong to the routine white-collar and blue-collar groups, are willing suburbanites for whom the cosmopolitan, upper-middle-class, inner-city culture has little or no meaning. These people find in suburbia the embodiment of a life style they desired before they settled there, and are reasonably content there. Many points that uppr-middle-class planners dislike about suburban life styles they regard either as not particularly disadvantageous (for instance, long commuter journeys) or positively advantageous (for instance, low-density housing). They are happy in the Levittowns and similar developments, and there is no evidence that they want much more. More ambitious, privately financed community projects, on the model of the new towns at Reston and Columbia, seem destined to meet the needs of a higher-income group who demand a better quality of communal service than the mass suburb can provide.[86] On the other hand, it must be said that the more limited research in Europe indicates that people may well be equally satisfied in different sorts of suburbia, at higher densities and with different qualities of urbanity.

Second, the very striking similarities in the economic organization of new American and Swedish suburbs indicate that at a given level of affluence, whatever the social system, people's demands for shopping and other urban services will express themselves very similarly. As populations suburbanize, their demands will produce a hierarchy of suburban centers supplying a rather standardized range of goods and services to populations up to the range 100,000-250,000. More specialized, and by definition less-common needs will be met in the metropolitan center of the suburban system, which will not decline but which may tend to stagnate while the suburban centers expand rapidly to cater to their growing populations.

Third, given the need for this hierarchy, it may be supplied in very different physical ways. There may be completely new, motorized, regional shopping centers, isolated from suburban areas and served from freeways, as in certain North American suburbs. There may be regional centers surrounded by high-density housing and linked both to mass transportation lines, as in the Stockholm suburbs. There may be progressive development of old market towns to serve growing suburban populations, as in the ring of countryside around London. There seems to be no evidence whatsoever that people prefer one kind of center rather than another; and indeed it would be difficult to supply, since in most countries people are familiar only with one kind of suburban center. On the other hand, there is some evidence that restructuring of existing centers is more costly than the building of new centers designed for easy access by car and for flexibility in growth. The case for this latter type of center will therefore depend on the unproven assumption that it generates more urban excitement than the new center.

One thing is certain: despite the pooling and exchange of international experience, and despite the common features of social and economic evolution that I have mentioned, metropolitan growth will take different forms in different countries, depending on tradition, history, local political forces, and the predilections of planners and officials. Looking to the future, to the end of the century, and projecting forward the main features of evolution in North America and in Europe, I see the following differentiation evolving.

On the one side there will be the European pattern of metropolitan growth. This will come in one respect closer to the American pattern, in that it will shed much of the impractical restrictionism which marked plans like that of Abercrombie for London in 1944 or the PADOG plan for Paris in 1960. Plans like these, which depended on fixed notion of urban form and on a rigid fence around the city as it had evolved at one point in time, are no longer acceptable in a context of growing population and rising income levels, with concomitant demands for space. The emphasis will now be on a flexible form of planning, which will channel urban growth in order to achieve certain stated planning goals, but which can adapt itself to changing economic and social circumstances. This new approach, termed *systems planning,* has become possible only in the last decade with the advance in electronic computers, which make it possible to digest and analyze a greater amount of complex data than was earlier thought possible.

But the liberation from rigid forms does not mean that planning can divorce itself from the notion of form. By definition, metropolitan planning is about the disposition of people and activities in space. We are likely, therefore, to see the evolution of a new form of plan, already presaged in Europe by the revised 1965 Plan for the Paris region, of the 1966 regional plan for the Greater Stockholm. These plans show a remarkable similarity in some of their basic features. They provide for future urban growth to take place along certain corridors of high-speed transportation, which commonly radiate outwards from the metropolitan centers and its surrounding agglomeration but which may take other forms—as in Paris, where two parallel areas of growth run east and west, linking with the suburbs of the existing agglomeration. Within the corridors of growth, urbanization will take place around certain nodes or subregional centers, each providing a range of urban services .and a considerable amount of employment for the surrounding population. The nodes will be linked with each other, especially in a radial direction along the urban corridors but to a certain extent by cross-connections between the corridors; and the density of traffic along the corridors is thought sufficient to justify rail-based mass transportation, as well as expressway links. Away from the main corridors of movement, densities of employment and of people will fall; thus everyone will have choice between the greater urban qualities of accessibility to employment, to services, and to transportation, and the suburban qualities of lower densities and better access to open space. At the outer edges of the lowest density areas, and therefore in the interstices between the corridors themselves, open space will be preserved for outdoor recreation. Because it is less accessible, this space will be subject to less pressure for urbanization; so that the form of the future metropolis will to some degree be self-regulating.

Such notions are found not only in Europe, but in the plans produced by one or two major metropolitan areas on the North American continent also. The concept of growth corridors, for instance, features prominently in the well-known Washington Year 2000 plan of 1960 and in the more recent plan for the Northeast Illinois Planning Commission for the Chicago metropolitan area. But up to now, it must be said that even these flexible notions of metropolitan region planning have been difficult to transplant to American soil. There is increasingly disturbing evidence that Washington Plan is being negated by building in contravention of the basic principles of corridor growth, simply because of the lack of effective planning powers on the metropolitan region level and the reluctance of local county governments to cooperate in proposals which may not suit their own interests. In addition, the capital investment has not yet been forthcoming for the mass transportation projects, which are an integral and essential feature of the corridor growth strategy.

The Washington experience, I think, illustrates an important general principle. In the absence of some quite new and radical political initiative, at either federal or state level, it seems certain that for the immediate future American metropolitan areas will continue to grow in ways quite different from their European counterparts. Their suburban areas will sprawl at increasingly low densities, with much leap-frogging over vacant land. They will be served hardly at all by mass transportation, almost exclusively by the private automobile. They will have a multinuclear structure, which will focus not on existing urban settlements that are to be swallowed up in the process of metropolitan growth, but on new regional shopping centers developed by private agencies and served by car. As suburbs recede ever farther from existing metropolitan downtown centers, it seems likely that these suburban centers will be called upon increasingly to supply a range of goods and services now only to be found downtown. This in turn will further weaken the prospects for mass transportation, which is only likely to be viable where supported by dense traffic along a few selected radial routes.

Thus, in the metropolitan future, the vital difference between the old, European urban culture and the new, American suburban culture will still survive. Though Europe will progressively suburbanize, it will do so within guidelines set by metropolitan regional plans, with a greater emphasis on higher residential densities, the preservation of existing urban centers (above all the metropolitan downtown), and the development of strong mass transportation links. In contrast, North America will increasingly see the growth of vast, low density, multi-nuclear suburbs owing little or nothing to past urban forms and linked together by cross-currents of automobile traffic.

Unless he is a dogmatist, the planner should welcome this diversity in metropolitan structure. For despite the recent advances in simulation models for urban development, there is still no urban laboratory like the urban area itself. The likelihood is that both types of metropolis will work; that both will offer specific advantages and specific disadvantages. The European metropolis will offer variation in living styles, in transportation modes, in types of urban experience; it will give its citizens a better exposure to unspoiled open countryside. But it is likely to be rather less flexible in coping with new and unforeseen needs and above all in coping with the pressures of the private automobile in leisure-time living. The American metropolis will offer a greater standardization and homogeneity of residential styles, shopping patterns, and visual experience; it will probably offer a higher level of accessibility by private car at the expense of an almost total lack of mass transportation. Probably its greatest deficiency will be its inability to provide for future open space demands within reasonable daily weekend reach of metropolitan areas; though this could be mitigated to some degree by a positive policy of reserving land for national and state park systems.

And it is very doubtful whether, in either case, most of the population will be other than completely satisfied with their various suburban modes of life. The question then is whether the planner has the responsibility to offer them something a little better than the bundle of goods they know and trust already. My personal answer is that if he has any responsibility other than that to produce an environment which is healthy and which functions with reasonable efficiency, the planner's task is to offer explicit choice: choice of housing styles, shopping styles, recreational styles, above and beyond what is commonplace and accepted. In this sense, despite the danger of inflexibility, I think the European metropolis may increasingly have lessons to teach the American. But this enhanced choice for the individual can only be achieved, paradoxically, through a greater degree of positive intervention by government agencies in the whole process of metropolitan growth.

NOTES

1. Lloyd R. Rodwin, *The British New Towns Policy: Problems and Implications* (Cambridge, Mass., 1956), *passim;* Peter Hall, *London 2000* (London, 1963), *passim;* Peter Hall, *The World Cities* (London, 1966), Chapter 2.

2. Peter Hall, "Planning for Urban Growth: Metropolitan Urban Plans and Their Implications for South-East England," *Regional Studies,* I (1967), p. 100.

3. Leonardo Benevolo, *The Origins of Modern Town Planning* (London, 1967), pp. 105-111.

4. Walter P. Webb, *The Great Plains* (Boston, 1931), Chapters 7-9.

5. Tom Wolfe, *The Kandy Kolored Tangerine Flake Streamline Baby* (London, 1966), pp. 10-11.

6. Lewis Mumford, *The Culture of Cities* (London, 1938), p. 8.

7. William H. Whyte, "Urban Sprawl," in *The Exploding Metropolis* (New York, 1958), p. 117.

8. Samuel E. Wood and Alfred E. Heller, *California Going, Going . . .* (Sacramento, 1962).

9. Lewis Mumford, *op. cit.,* p. 397.

10. Ian Nairn, *The American Landscape: A Critical View* (New York, 1965), p. 13.

11. Morton and Lucia White, *The Intellectual Versus the City* (Cambridge, Mass., 1962), p. 201.

12. P. Blake, *Frank Lloyd Wright: Architecture and Space* (London, 1963), p. 12.

13. Frank Lloyd Wright, *An Autobiography* (London, 1945), p. 281-282.

14. Frank Lloyd Wright, *When Democracy Builds* (London, 1945), p. 66.

15. Reyner Banham, "Brown Angels a Go Go," *New Society,* VIII 1966), p. 199.

16. James E. Vance, Jr., "Geography and Urban Evolution in the San Francisco Bay Area," in *The San Francisco Bay Area: Its Probems and Future* (Berkeley, 1964), II, pp. 68-69.

17. Robert B. Riley, "Urban Myths and the New Cities of the South-West," *Landscape,* XVII (1967), p. 21.

18. Melvin Webber, "Order in Diversity: Community Without Propinquity," in *Cities and Space: The Future Use of Urban Form,* ed. Lowdon Wingo, Jr. (Baltimore, 1963), p. 52.

19. Robert M. Haig, "Toward an Understanding of the Metropolis. II. The Assignment of Activities to Areas in Urban Regions," *Quarterly Journal of Economics*, XL (1925-1926), p. 427.

20. Edgar M. Hoover and Raymond Vernon, *Anatomy of a Metropolis* (Cambridge, Mass., 1959), pp. 89 and 101; Louis B. Schlivek, *Man in Metropolis* (Garden City, N.Y., 1965), *passim*.

21. Webber, *op. cit.*, p. 46.

22. Riley, *op. cit.*, p. 22.

23. Melvin Webber, "The Urban Place and the Nonplace Urban Realm," in *Explorations into Urban Structure*, ed. Webber et al. (Philadelphia, 1964), *passim*.

24. David Riesman, "The Suburban Dislocation," *Annals of the American Academy of Political and Social Science*, CCCXIV (November 1957), p. 134.

25. *Ibid.*, p. 133.

26. *Ibid.*, p. 132.

27. William H. Whyte, "The Anti-City," in *Man and the Modern City*, ed. Elizabeth Geen et al. (Pittsburgh, 1962), pp. 46-47.

28. Louis Wirth, "Urbanization as a Way of Life," *American Journal of Sociology*, XLIV (1938), pp. 12, 16, 17, *et passim*.

29. Robert E. Park, Ernest W. Burgess, and Roderick D. McKenzie, *The City* (Chicago, 1925, 1967), p. 51.

30. *Ibid.*, p. 23.

31. Herbert J. Gans, *The Urban Villagers* (New York, 1962), p. 15.

32. Michael Young and Peter Willmott, *Family and Kinship in East London* (London, 1957), p. 156.

33. Gans. *op. cit.*, p. 4.

34. *Ibid.*, pp. 242-243.

35. *Ibid.*, p. 268.

36. *Ibid.*, p. 16.

37. Herbert J. Gans, "Urbanism and Suburbanism as Ways of Life: A Re-valuation of Definitions," in *Human Behavior and Social Progress: An Interactionist Approach*, ed. Arnold M. Rose (New York, 1962), p. 634.

38. Morris Janowitz, *The Community Press in an Urban Setting* (Glencoe, Ill., 1952), pp. 140-141.

39. Ernest R. Mowrer, "The Family in Suburbia," in *The Suburban Community*, ed. William M. Dobriner (New York, 1958), pp. 155-156.

40. Hoover and Vernon, *op. cit.*, p. 202.

41. Harold L. Wattel, "Levittown: A Suburban Community," in *The Suburban Community*, ed. William Dobriner (New York, 1958), pp. 290, 296, 304.

42. Edward P. Eichler and Marshall Kaplan, *The Community Builders* (Berkeley, 1967), p. 171, quoting Weaver.

43. Bennett Berger, *Working Class Suburb: A Study of Auto Workers in Suburbia* (Berkeley, 1960), pp. 15-25, 58-59, 65.

44. William H. Whyte, *The Organization Man* (London, 1958).

45. John Seeley et al., *Crestwood Heights* (Toronto, 1956).

46. Wattel, *op. cit.*

47. Berger, *op. cit.*, pp. 91-92.

48. *Ibid.*, p. 103.

49. Herbert J. Gans, *The Levittowners: Ways of Life and Politics in a New Suburban Community* (London, 1967), p. 288.

50. *Ibid.*, p. 417.

51. Herbert J. Gans, "Planning and Social Life: An Evaluation of Friendship and Neighborhood Patterns in Suburban Communities," *Journal of the American Institute of Planners*, XXVII (1961), p. 139.

52. Herbert J. Gans, "The Balanced Community: Homogeneity or Heterogeneity in Residential Areas," *Journal of the American Institute of Planners*, XXVII (1961), pp. 291-292.

53. *Ibid.*, p. 293.

54. Christen T. Jonassen, *The Shopping Center Versus Downtown* (Columbus, Ohio, 1955), p. 95.

55. *Ibid.*, pp. 97-100.

56. James E. Vance, Jr., "Emerging Patterns of Commercial Structure in American Cities," in *Proceedings of the IGU Symposium on Urban Geography, Lund, 1960,* ed. Knut Norborg. Lund Studies in Geography, Series B., No. 24 (1962), p. 517.

57. Brian J. L. Berry et al., *Commercial Structure and Commercial Blight,* University of Chicago, Department of Geography, Research Paper No. 85 (Chicago, 1963), p. 29.

58. *Ibid.*, p. 27.

59. J. R. Meyer, J. F. Kain, and M. Wohl, *The Urban Transportation Probem* (Cambridge, Mass., 1965), p. 54.

60. *Ibid.*, pp. 42-43.

61. Folke Kristensson, "The Impact of Changing Ecological and Organizational Structure on Urban Core Development (Size and Structure), in *Urban Core and Inner City,* Sociographical Department, University of Amsterdam (Leiden, 1967), pp. 4, 8-9.

62. Berry et al., *op. cit.,* p. 60, quoting Voorhees.

63. William L. Garrison et al., *Studies of Highway Development and Geographic Change* (Seattle, 1959), pp. 46-49; Berry et al., *op. cit.,* p. 60.

64. Garrison et al., *op. cit.,* p. 48.

65. Berry et al., *op. cit.,* p. 49.

66. Vance, *op. cit.,* p. 512.

67. Peter Hall, "Planning for Urban Growth: Metropolitan Urban Plans and Their Implications for South-East England," *op. cit.*

68. Garrison et al., pp. 137-138.

69. G. A. Wissink, *American Cities in Perspective, with Special Reference to the Development of Their Fringe Areas* (Assen, Netherlands, 1962), p. 49.

70. August Lösch, *The Economics of Location,* tr. William H. Woglom (New Haven, 1954), pp. 124-127.

71. Patricia Ellman, "Report of the Socio-Geographic Inquiry." London School of Economics, Greater London Group, Report to the Royal Commission on Local Government in England. (Mimeographed.)

72. Gerald Manners, "Some Costs of Urban Growth: Implications for South-East Wales," *Town and Country Planning,* XXXIII (1965), p. 80.

73. Aubrey M. Diem, "An Alternative to Unplanned Urban Growth: The Case of Stockholm," *Canadian Geographer,* IX (1965), p. 200.

74. Jane Jacobs, *The Death and Life of Great American Cities* (London, 1962), *passim.*

75. William F. Heinemeyer, "The Urban Core as a Centre of Attraction." Studyweek Urban Core and Inner City, Amsterdam, September 1966. (Mimeographed.)

76. *Ibid.*, pp. 89-90.

77. H. D. De Vries Reilingh, "The Tension Between Form and Function in the Inner City of Amsterdam." Studyweek Urban Core and Inner City, Amsterdam, September 1966. (Mimeographed.)

78. Whyte, *Urban Sprawl, op. cit.,* pp. 7-9.

79. Paul Ylvisacker, "The Shape of the Future: Urban Life," in *Metropolis: Values in Conflict,* ed. C. E. Elias, Jr., James Gilles, and Svend Riener (Belmont, Calif., 1961), p. 67.

80. John E. Burchard, "The Limitations of Utilitarianism as a Basis for Determining Urban Joy," in *Man and the Modern City,* ed. Elizabeth Geen et al. (Pittsburgh, 1962), p. 18.

81. Gans, *The Levittowners, op. cit.,* p. 425.

82. Wolfe, *op cit.,* pp. 7-8.

83. Banham, *op. cit.,* pp. 331-332.

84. Kevin Lynch, *The Image of the City* (Cambridge, Mass., 1960), pp. 41-42.

85. *Ibid.*, passim.

86. Eichler and Kaplan, *op. cit.,* Chapter 6.

6

James W. Rouse

Cities That Work for Man

Nearly one-half of all the people in the United States in the year 2000 will live in dwelling units that have not yet been started and on land that has not yet been broken (and the year 2000 is not so far away—as close in our future as the year 1934 in our past).

Every month in the United States we are adding roughly 300,000 people, a city the size of Toledo.

Every year we add a new Philadelphia.

In twenty years we will double the size of Los Angeles and the San Francisco Bay area. We will add 6,000,000 people to the New York region in the same period.

Since 1940 Baltimore has added to its population a city larger than Milwaukee. In the next twenty years it will add another city about the size of Miami. And in the same period of time Washington, 35 miles away, will be adding a city nearly as large as Baltimore.

Such are the dynamics of our urban growth. It has been said that in the remainder of this century we will build, new, in our cities, the equivalent of all that has been built since Plymouth Rock.

What opportunity this represents! Opportunity for business, for jobs, for the development of new and better institutions to serve our people. And opportunity to plan and develop this new one-half of our American cities free of the mistakes of the past, responsive to the needs of the future.

How are we handling this opportunity? How are we shaping the growth of our cities? Not very well. Our cities grow by sheer chance—by accident, by whim of the private developer and public agencies. A farm is sold and begins raising houses instead of potatoes, then another farm. Forests are cut; valleys are filled; streams are buried in storm sewers. Kids overflow the schools; a new school is built. Churches come up out of the basements. Then more schools, more churches. Traffic grows; roads are widened, front yards cut back. Service stations, Tastee-Freez, hamburger stands pockmark the old highway. Traffic is strangled; an expressway is hacked through the landscape; then a cloverleaf, a regional shopping center, office buildings, high-rise apartments—and so it goes.

Thus, the bits and pieces of a city are splattered across the landscape. By this irrational process, noncommunities are born—formless places without order, beauty or reason, with no visible respect for people or the land. Thousands of small separate decisions made with little or no relationship to one another, nor to their composite impact, produce a major decision about the future of our cities and our civilization—a decision we have come to label suburban sprawl. What nonsense this is! What reckless, irresponsible dissipation of nature's endowment and of man's hope for dignity, beauty, growth!

Sprawl is inefficient. It stretches out the distances people must travel to work, to shop, to worship, to play. It fails to relate these activities in ways that strengthen each, and thus it suppresses values that orderly relationships and concentration of uses would stimulate. Sprawl is ugly, oppressive, massively dull. It squanders the resources of nature—forests, streams, hillsides—and produces vast, monotonous armies of housing and graceless, tasteless clutter. But worst of all, sprawl is inhuman. It is antihuman. The vast formless spread of housing pierced by the unrelated spotting of schools, churches, stores, creates areas so huge and irrational that they are out of scale with people, beyond their grasp and comprehension, too big for people to feel a part of, responsible for, important in.

And we know how to do it so much better. We know the rough measurements of the future growth of every metropolitan area in the country. We know about how many people we must provide for—how many houses and apartments, how many schools, how many churches, how many stores we must build. We know that we must build the sewer lines, water lines, roads and highways to serve this growth. And we know how to relate houses, churches, schools, stores, employment centers to one another in healthy, human, rational communities that respect both man and nature, and in which business can prosper.

Yet it is fair to say that not one single metropolitan area in the United States has a comprehensive plan for its future growth and development that will accommodate the growth it *knows will occur* in communities that will provide what it *knows ought to be*. We improvise frantically and impulsively with each new thrust of growth as if it were a gigantic surprise—beyond our capacity to predict or to manage. Is there any other aspect of American life in which the gap is so wide between our knowledge and our performance as in the growth of the American city? We can plan to visit the moon; develop new technology to carry out the plan; advance the technology to the reality of flight in space. And soon we will put man on the moon. Yet, so far, we have been unable or unwilling to put to effective use the knowledge that is commonplace among us, to shape the orderly growth of our cities into communities that are in scale with people; responsive to their needs and yearnings and sensitive to the landscape we invade. Why is this so? Why do we, as a nation with such proven capacity for systematically organizing a production task, persist in this disorderly, unsystematic, inefficient building of cities? There are several reasons, and they must be understood if the city of the future is to provide a better life for its people than the city of the past.

One reason is that there is the state of mind about the American city. We have lived so long with grim, congested, worn-out inner cities and sprawling, cluttered outer cities that we have come, subconsciously, to accept them as inevitable and unavoidable. Deep down in our national heart is a lack of conviction that cities can be beautiful, humane, and truly responsive to the needs and yearnings of our people. Sprawl is thought to be better than slum because it is greener, cleaner, and less crowded. We accept the deficits of noncommunity; the scatteration of facilities, the frantic, fractured living, the loneliness amidst busyness, the rising delinquency among middle-class children, increasing neurosis, alcoholism, divorce; the destruction of nature and the dull monotonous man-made replacement. We accept it all as if it were a preordained way of life beyond our capacity to significantly influence, shape, or control. Lacking images of urban growth in communities that are in human scale and sensitive to both man and nature, we take what the developer gives us and we think we have to like it.

A second reason is that we lack the organized capacity in America, at the present time, to produce well-planned new communities. Although the city-building business is the largest single industry in the United States, we have grown no General Motors, no IBM, in city building. We build our cities—houses, apartments, business and industry—through small corporate enterprises, no one of which has the capacity to undertake, out of its own resources, the research and development investment required to produce new communities that will match our knowledge and our needs. City building has been largely an ad hoc enterprise—the purchase of a small tract of land, building and marketing a piece of a city. Whereas there is a handful of automobile manufacturers and perhaps a few dozen office equipment producers who spend hundreds of millions of dollars in scientific research to produce better automobiles and typewriters, the building of our cities is divided among thousands of small enterprises and there is almost no research and little private planning for the most important product we produce—the American city.

Responsibility for city building has not only been divided among thousands of small underequipped businesses, it has also been shared uncertainly with local government. We have assigned to the counties, townships, and cities the basic responsibility for urban planning, but we have failed to demand that these local governments carry out their plans, and we have failed to give them the authority to do so. Metropolitan planning throughout America proceeds in an atmosphere of unreality, fancy, disbelief. Except for highways and public utilities, urban planning seldom carries with it the reality of programs to be executed. The result is loose-jointed, broad-brush planning of land uses, which easily gives way to the pressure of piecemeal development economics or to local politics.

A third reason is that the steps that might be taken to produce well-conceived new communities and establish new images to stimulate larger corporate enterprise and more effective local government action are restrained by popular myths that hold that it is not possible to do what needs to be done. These myths say: "Our system of private property rights and chopped-up ownership of land makes it impossible to assemble under single ownership the land required for comprehensive community planning and development." Or: "Even if it were possible to buy the land, it would be impossible to find financing for its acquisition and development. This would take millions of dollars. No one is willing to put up that kind of dough." Or: "Even if you could buy the land and raise the money to pay for it and develop it, you could never get the zoning. Local people and politicians will clobber you when you try." Or: "If you are lucky enough to get the land, the financing, and the zoning, you will go broke trying to build a really fine community. The arithmetic won't work. The cost of providing a good community will eat you up. People won't pay for it."

This, then, is the mood with which we face the building of a new America over the next three decades. Right now we are compounding the mistakes of the past as we build large parts of our nation into an infinite Los Angeles. Along the East Coast, in the North Central region, on the West Coast, and in parts of the South and Southwest, cities sprawl out towards one another in formless, cluttered growth that has been labeled megalopolis. This ominous word carries with it threatening overtones that people, families, and all hope for rational and humane community will be lost in massive, monotonous sprawl.

Against this background, may I report to you on an experience in city building that is exploding some of the myths that have trapped our state of mind about the city. It is the story of Columbia, a new city midway between Baltimore and Washington. Our business is mortgage banking and real estate development. Across the United States our company finances apartments, shopping centers, office and industrial buildings built by hundreds of real estate developers. Also, as developer, we build, own, and manage such properties for our own account. Thus, we have been elaborately involved in the "bits and pieces" approach to city building. Perceiving from this platform the damage and deficits of disordered growth and observing also the important gains in convenience, community life, and economic value that occur when the pieces of city are arranged in constructive relationship to one another, we began to ask ourselves questions such as: Why not build a whole new city? Couldn't houses and apartments, schools and churches, business and industry be so arranged in relationship to one another that each would give strength and value to the other? Couldn't all of this be fit on the land, to dignify and ennoble it, instead of to destroy it? Couldn't hills and forests and stream valleys be respected and used to give shape, separation, and identity to communities within the city? Couldn't such a city be not only more beautiful and more human but also more profitable to build?

Prodded by the answers to our own questions, we built a hypothetical model of a complete small city. We found that it made sense. So we focused on the area midway between Washington and Baltimore to see if it could be made real. Our target was a city of 100,000. It would take 14,000 acres of land, with a probable land cost of $20-25 million. This was far beyond our available resources and probably too much for any developer in America. Thus, we appealed to a great financial institution that we had represented for twenty years as mortgage loan correspondent—the Connecticut General Life Insurance Company. We believed then and now that there was a special compatibility between public purpose and private profit in producing a well-planned new city. But never, to our knowledge, had a major life insurance company entered the city-building process at this early stage and on the scale and in the manner this required. We asked Connecticut General to provide the funds to acquire the land and to participate with us in the venture as a co-owner of the project. We agreed to supply the funds for planning and predevelopment administration. In a remarkable, perhaps historic, act of financial statesmanship, Connecticut General joined us in the venture. They committed what proved to be $25 million for the purchase and early carrying charges on 15,600 acres of land.

In February 1963, we commenced our acquisition program. By October 1963, we had completed the purchase of 14,000 acres and appeared before the county commissioners of Howard County to disclose our acquisition and our purpose to build a city. We commenced planning in the fall of 1963 amidst great skepticism and anxiety among our neighbors in the county. Our only reassurance to them could be that we were at their mercy. Unless we produced a plan that they found better than the prospect of scattered, sprawling growth, protected by half-acre zoning, they would reject our proposal and deny us zoning. Thus, it was up to us to prove that we could plan a city that would constitute, in fact, a better alternative to sprawl.

We set four main objectives in our planning:

1. *To build a real city—not just a better suburb, but a complete new city.* There will be business and industry to establish a sound economic base, roughly 30,000 jobs, and houses and apartments at rents and prices to match the income of all who work there, from company janitor to company executive. Provision will be made for schools and churches, for libraries, college, hospital, concert halls, theaters, restaurants, hotels, offices, and department stores. Like any real city of 100,000, Columbia will be economically diverse, polycultural, multifaith, and interracial.

2. *To respect the land.* On sets of transparent overlays we recorded the topography, the stream valleys, the forests, the historic buildings, the special vistas, the quiet tree-lined lanes. We invited the land to impose itself as a discipline on the form of the community.

Columbia will provide 3,200 acres of open spaces, parks, recreation areas, and five small new lakes. The three major stream valleys will be preserved, along with 3,000 acres of forests. These green areas will interlace the entire community, separating and connecting the nine villages and leading into the heart of downtown, which will have a 50-acre forest on one side and a lake on another.

3. *To provide the best possible environment for the growth of people.* Here is the heart of the planning process—to plan out from the needs and yearnings of people to the kind of community that will best serve and nourish their growth. But how to do it? If you want to know about the needs of people, about what seems to work well for people or badly, where do you go? Whom do you ask? Architects, engineers, planners, bankers, and developers are not the people who work intimately with people. Why not go to teachers and ministers and doctors, to psychiatrists, psychologists, and social scientists to plan a city? We are an extensively examined society. There is enormous knowledge about our growth and development as people, of our success and failure, our hopes and fears; and yet it is knowledge that is almost never brought to bear in the process of community planning. There is no dialogue between the people engaged in urban design and development and the behavioral sciences. Why not? Why not bring together a group of people who would know about people from a variety of backgrounds and experiences to view the prospect of a new city and shed light on how it might be made to work best for the people who would live there?

Thus, we convened a "work group" of fourteen men and women for that purpose: an eminent social scientist; a psychiatrist from the Department of Public Health at Johns Hopkins; a sociologist who worked for two years in Levittown, New Jersey; a psychologist from the University of Michigan with a rich awareness of the art of communication and its roadblocks; a city manager; a commissioner of recreation; a sociologist in consumer behavior research from the General Electric Company; a woman concerned with the status of women; a political scientist; an economist; an educator; and others.

154

This work group and our architects and planners met together every two weeks for two days and a night, for six months. We were not seeking a blueprint for a Utopian society. We did not want a report, a recommendation, or even agreement. We wanted conversation in depth about man, his family and his institutions. We wanted to allow these insights about people to influence the physical plan and to guide us in stimulating within the community the kinds of programs in school, church, health, culture, recreation, and work that would support the growth of people. Together we examined the optimums. What would be the best possible school system in a city of 100,000, the best health system? How might religion be made most effective in the growth of people? With shorter work weeks and increasing wages, what opportunities can be made available for better use of leisure time? How can music, art, theater, adult education, physical recreation be made available most usefully to the people in the city? Can the relationship of home, school, church, and community be such that there is some alternative to loneliness, relief from fear, and growth from hate? In what size neighborhoods do people feel most comfortable? In what kind of community are they the most effectively challenged, the most creative? What about homogeneity and heterogeneity? What would all these questions and these answers say about the plan for a new city? We did not worry at the moment about feasibility. It would compromise us soon enough.

It was a thrilling and productive process. All of us who are working on Columbia feel enriched and strengthened by it. By seeking out the best we could conceive for people and by opening our minds to those possibilities, we leaped over many roadblocks which conventional wisdom had declared to be unmovable.

4. *To make a profit.* This was no residual goal—not something just to be hoped for as a possibility. It was and is a prime objective. The profit purpose was alive and creative throughout the planning process. It was using the marketplace to cast votes for what people really want and care about enough to pay for. It recognized the dynamics of the market system as being fundamental to the democratic process, for it

is through the marketplace that a free people can best make the complex judgments of how, where, and when they wish to spend their earnings. A continuing examination of profitability is simply a responsible attempt to perceive the marketplace votes and respond to them. It moderates the temptation toward imposing one's own bias on others. It resists the pull toward sentimentality, sophistication, and arrogance. It hauls dreams into focus with reality and leads to bone and muscle solution. It gives integrity to the ultimate plan.

Columbia, by producing an outstanding profit, will speak loud and clear to the city-building industry. It will induce attention to a good environment as the right product in city building. It will warn against the unmarketability of sprawl. It will lift attention to genuine respect for nature and the family. Failure, or even moderate success, would be a blow to better hopes for urban growth. It would support the myth that it is not economic to produce a good environment.

By the fall of 1964 the plan was completed and presented to the people and the county government of Howard County. A sketch of Columbia would show a small city consisting of nine villages or small towns with 10,000 to 15,000 people each, around a downtown core. This system of villages that we call a city stretches nine miles east and west, and roughly five miles north and south along U. S. 29, which bisects the land area. The villages are separated by stream valleys, parks, and bridle paths that lace through the city. They are served by Columbia's bus system, which will run on its own right-of-way, connecting the village centers, the major employment centers, and downtown. Forty per cent of the families will live within a few minutes' walk of the bus line.

A village will consist of four to six neighborhoods of 500 to 700 families each. At the center of each neighborhood is an elementary school, a community room, child care center, playground, swimming pool, and a small store that is a cross between a neighborhood drug store and a country grocery store. A path system separated from the roads will make the neighborhood center easily accessible as a neighborhood meeting place for teachers, parents, children, and their friends. Even little kids will be able to walk to school without fighting the automobile.

The neighborhoods cluster around a village center where there is brought together in a single place the facilities that, typically today, are splattered across the landscape. High school, middle school, library, auditorium, churches, medical clinic; together with supermarket, service stores, and gasoline service station are grouped around a village green to provide a lively center for the 10,000 to 15,000 people in the village. Thus, teachers, parents and kids, ministers, merchants, doctors and patients—all the people of a village—engage one another in the daily course of life. The opportunity is created to meet and know one another; to share problems; to communicate yearnings.

The path system feeds into the village center by underpasses that allow kids to ride bikes; older people to walk; mothers to push baby carriages into the heart of the village life. The physical plan emancipates men, women, and children to a wider range of choices and a richer variety of life.

How many children in the massive sprawl around our big cities can walk or ride a bike to school, a library, or a music lesson, to a stream to fish or to a lake to sail, to a store, the movies, or the theater? The choices will be available in Columbia by foot, bike, or bus. And it takes no miracle or subsidy to do it—simply thoughtful planning over a large enough land area to account for the things that people want and need to live a full and enriching life.

At the heart of Columbia, serving all its people, will be the town center with department stores and specialty shops, restaurants, movies, theater, concert hall, offices, hotels, a college, a hospital, the main library, and a town center park and lake. It will be a beautiful, lively, efficient downtown.

A number of myths have already been exploded: The land was assembled; the financing was arranged; the zoning was obtained. A new economic model is completed each quarter, projecting the cost and the income of developing Columbia to completion. The economics have not yet been proven, but the progress is encouraging and there is sound reason to believe that we will be able to prove that it is more profitable to build a good environment than a bad one.

It is the size and scale of Columbia and the comprehensiveness of the planning that has exploded these myths. The planning showed the people of Howard County that stream valleys and forests could be preserved; that a wide range of recreational, cultural, and educational facilities could be provided; that places to work and shop could be brought conveniently close at hand; and, perhaps most important, that a balanced growth of business along with housing would provide a sounder base for taxes to support the cost of government. Thus, in a county that was fighting mad about the ravages of urban sprawl and aroused by tumultuous zoning battles, Columbia offered a better alternative. At the crucial hearing on Columbia's original zoning proposal, not a single resident of the county appeared in opposition.

The prospect of a new city, the opportunity to build from scracth in a new environment, has stimulated a wonderfully creative response in the schools and churches, in health and culture:

1. County school boards, facing random, surging growth, are largely committed to big, consolidated schools because they have no other choice. They must locate schools where they will be accessible to the developments as they pop up—unplanned and unscheduled. The children are bussed in. But in Columbia we have been able to lay out for the next fifteen years the school sites for this part of Howard County. The School Board has accepted the concept of neighborhood and village schools. The elimination of school busses alone is estimated to save over a million dollars per year, at current busing costs, by 1980.

Stimulated by the prospect of new possibilities in education, a special study has been made for the Howard County School Board by Drs. Anderson of Harvard and Alexander of Florida. This report focuses attention on the importance of developing the child as an individual. It proposes ungraded schools, team teaching, and other programs intended to strengthen and update the educational effort in Howard County. The Ford Foundation offers grants to the Howard County

School Board to design new elementary and middle schools that will be responsive to the new curriculum proposals. The first of these is now under construction in Columbia's first neighborhood. The Howard County School Board has announced that the Howard County community college will be located in the heart of downtown Columbia. This institution is expected to offer a wide range of adult education and vocational training programs to the community, as well as the first two years of college to high school graduates.

2. Twelve major Protestant denominations have joined together in a program without precedent in America. They have formed a Religious Facilities Corporation, which will own all the church buildings in Columbia, thus eliminating competition for church status and permitting large-scale economies through multiple use of facilities. They plan joint centers of religious instruction and joint mission efforts on both a local and a world basis. The ministers will belong to a Cooperative Ministry, sharing staff and joining forces in programs of counseling and service to the community. Cardinal Shehan has announced the interest of the Catholic Archdiocese in joining the Protestants in the Religious Facilities Corporation so that Catholic and Protestant churches will jointly own and share facilities. Catholics, Protestants, and Jews have formed the Columbia Interfaith Housing Corporation to build and rent housing to low-income families.

3. The Johns Hopkins Medical School and Hospital has announced its interest in establishing a comprehensive health care system for Columbia residents. A study to determine economic feasibility is now under way. If the announced hopes of the study are fulfilled, this great medical institution will provide on a monthly payment basis to Columbia residents a comprehensive system of health care from home nursing service to medical clinics to hospitalization, with extensive provision for community-wide health education. One of the prime purposes of this health system would be to test out the belief that a comprehensive system of health education, early diagnosis, and preventive medicine can be financially supported by the dollars saved

from hospitalization and crisis medical care. In other words, Columbia medicine will be working on the possibility that it costs no more to build a healthy community than to treat a sick one. This could be an important advance in medical and health systems in America.

4. Washington's National Symphony has signed a thirty-year contract to provide a minimum of twenty concerts a season in the Merriweather Post Pavilion of Music in the heart of downtown Columbia. This in turn has triggered a chain reaction of hopes and prospects in the field of music, theater, and art which hold out every prospect of a rich, cultural life in this new city.

5. Other studies and negotiations are under way with respect to the library system, communications, banking, transportation, and retailing which can result in important new steps in the services made available to the people of Columbia.

Each of these important and stimulating new hopes for Columbia is born out of what we have come to call "The Columbia Process." It is a process that begins with an honest attempt to learn what might work best for the people who will live there and then to discover by physical planning and by study and negotiation with leaders in the schools and churches, in the health, cultural, and recreation institutions how these hopes might best be achieved.

This process is fundamental to good planning and effective development, whether it be for the accommodation of outlying growth or for the renewal of the old worn-out inner city. The task is to produce a community—a community in which a man, his wife, and children are important, come first, ahead of buildings, streets, and automobiles; a community which, in physical form, they can identify, find boundaries to, feel responsible for and be proud of; a community which in human terms cares about them, suffers with them, prays for them.

The search for this kind of community will lead to questions and produce answers; it will generate plans that will work for people—different plans in different circumstances, but always plans to nourish and support the growth and dignity of the individual human being and his family. This is the only legitimate purpose for our cities or our civilization—to grow better people—people who are more concerned, inspired, fulfilled, more loving people.

We are living in the midst of what history may find to have been the most important revolution in the history of man. It is the upheaval that has lifted to new heights man's respect for the dignity and importance of his fellow man. Institutions that degrade man and barriers that separate men from one another are under relentless assault. Thus, the cold, grim oppressiveness of the scaleless, inhuman cities is under attack on many fronts. The individual skirmishes flare up in terms of bad housing, unemployment, crime, dope, delinquency, even riots. But these are only symptoms of a battle raging at much deeper levels that will be won by the building of new cities and, even more dramatically, by the rebuilding and restructuring of our older cities. The key will be "restructuring" in such manner that the city will support growth instead of working erosion in human personality. This new city will look different because it will be broken up by parks, open spaces, schools, playgrounds, and transportation systems into definable communities in which people are important. Together these communities will make up a new kind of city, dynamic and humane.

This revolution is barely under way. The tools for carrying it out have been forged over the past several decades. We are now developing the will to pick up the tools and put them to work. Over the next ten years, we will see an urban revolution that will lead all men—rich and poor, black and white—to take possession of their cities and make them work for the people who live there.

161

7

Constantinos A. Doxiadis

How to Build the City of the Future

We talk a great deal about our cities, about the bad conditions in them. We are beginning to talk about the cities of the future, but we seldom discuss the problem of how we should build the city of the future. This is the crucial question, because no matter what we say about how bad the cities of the present are—and they are bad; no matter what we say about the causes of the trouble we are in—and we are in trouble; no matter what dreams or plans we make for the city of the future, unless we face the problem of how to build the city of the future, we will never achieve anything. We will continue living under bad conditions in bad cities, and we will suffer more and more.

It is time for us to think about this problem in a systematic way and to face the big question of how to build the city of the future. In order to achieve this, we must pass through several stages that will help us to clarify our thinking. Such stages are: What is a city? What happens to our cities today? Why worry about the cities of the future? Then we must face the different alternatives for the future of our cities and turn to the big question: how we should build them. In order to answer this question we must first ask ourselves whether we can conceive the city of the future. If so, we must be able to conceive the future of every single one of our cities and then finally we must turn our minds onto how to realize, how to implement, how to build our conceptions. This is the task we have to undertake.

WHAT IS A CITY?

If we ask this question of any group of people taken at random, we will get completely different answers. I doubt if there will be two people who will give exactly the same answer. If we ask how big their city is, what the boundaries of the city are, how many people it contains, how satisfied they are, what the elements of the city are, we will certainly get different replies and this is quite natural.

Let us take the simple case of one family. We ask the father where his city is, what it is, how he likes it. He may well answer that his city is downtown, because that is where he has his business. His city is a big industrial town and he likes it very much; by this he probably means that it has a thriving business for him. If we ask the mother of the family the same questions, she may well answer that her city is not the big downtown area, but the outskirts where she lives, probably including the big shopping center that she visits quite often, her children's schools, and the area where most of her friends live. She may say that it is a residential city and that she does not like it at all. This may be because this suburb where she lives does not have the cultural facilities of a different suburb in a different city where they previously lived.

If we ask the son of the family, he may say that his city extends into the outskirts, it goes beyond downtown to the other side where his college is, which he attends daily. He may say that his city is a big city. By this he may mean that it is the best in the area and he is delighted by it. He may say that he likes it very much, and this may be because of the sports facilities that his broader urban area makes available to him. The same question, put to the daughter, may be answered as follows: the city is very small and very provincial. It is an unimportant urban area and she does not like it at all. By this she may mean that it does not offer any possibility of studying dancing and ballet, although she wants to dedicate her life to this. Her city, the whole urban area, does not satisfy her at all; she wants to move to a big metropolis. If we finally ask the grandmother, she may just say that her city is very small; she still thinks of what the city was in her youth when she married and she moved to this house where her son still lives with her. She may say that it is a quiet place, a quiet small city and she may add, "but it is the most beautiful city in the United States," and by this she means that the old elm trees planted a century ago in her street are still there and very beautiful as compared to the other streets where her friends live, which she dislikes because they are newly opened and without any trees at all. Five people give five replies and cannot agree on what a city is, and this is a basic reason for our confusion.

In fact, by "city" we mean many things, and we should not use the term *city* but only the term *human settlement*. The era when the city was a unit of a habitat very clearly defined in space has passed. Before the eighteenth century the city was even surrounded by walls; then, although the walls were not needed any longer it had a definite distinction from the countryside, there was a place where the city ended and the countryside began. This is no longer true. Our human settlements spread all around. The city has turned into a dynamic growing organism which, if it is big, absorbs in its growth the outlying small cities or villages and expands even beyond. If it is small, it spreads along some highways, along country roads. In this way the definition of the city either by size or by boundaries, and, because of this, even the definition of its contents, is very difficult. I think that it will be correct to speak of the city in the sense of all our human settlements in which we live, large and small, good and bad, and then try to differentiate by size, by units, by communities within broader areas, by neighborhoods, by streets, down to our single houses. In this way we will be able to say, and will be much more correct in saying, that we live in a big urban region, in a certain metropolis within it, in a certain suburb within such a community, such a neighborhood. We will be more correct in trying to clarify the specific unit we are referring to, and whether this satisfies us, and how much.

WHAT IS HAPPENING TO OUR CITIES?

If we have answered the question of what our city is, we should now ask ourselves why we should start worrying about our cities. What is actually happening to our cities today which did not happen before, allowing us to say that our cities are in a crisis? To understand this, we must look at the city in a systematic way in order to specify how much this city satisfies us in relation to the satisfaction we, or our ancestors, received from the city of the past.

To answer such a question we should not look at the city as a nondifferentiated whole, but should start looking at its parts and its elements. We have already mentioned one way in which we can look at the city in a systematic way by dividing it into parts. There are also other ways in which we can look at the city. The first is by its elements. The city consists of five elements: nature, for which it is built; man, who came into nature and started developing the human settlements and finally the cities; society, which has been formed by man; shells, that is all sorts of buildings and houses, from the small house to the big public buildings and factories built by society; and networks, roads, highways, railways, water supply and electrical systems, telecommunications, and so forth, which make the city function, which connect its parts.

We can also look at the whole city in different ways. We can look at it as an economic phenomenon or a social phenomenon, a political or administrative problem, a technological phenomenon, or finally, a cultural and aesthetic one. If we now try to combine these five elements of the city in the five basic ways in which we can study them, we may tend to say that there are twenty-five ways of looking at our problems. But such a conclusion is wrong, as the total of the combinations of the five elements seen in five ways leads to a figure considerably larger than 33,000,000. We can now see why each one of us gets a different image and opinion about his city. Somebody looks at it as an economic phenomenon, referring to the use of the land; somebody else as a social phenomenon related to the racial conditions, and so on.

No matter which way we look at the city, we will discover that it is in a crisis. If we have any doubt, we have only to think that nature is today much more mishandled than it was in the past. We spoil many more land resources than at any time in the past. In the last forty years only, in the United States and other countries which show the same trends, we have used three times as much land per capita than before.

In addition to this, we contaminate the air, we pollute the water to an unprecedented degree. So, if we look at the city from the point of view of the element, nature, we must say that we are now in a much worse condition than before. If we look at the city from the point of view of the single man and his values, we come to the same conclusions. We have only to think of a man at his home losing his privacy, suffering from much greater noise, and then a man in the street who is in grave danger, our children being killed by automobiles, everybody losing his personal freedom to cross the road, to use his square, to walk freely, to run, to enjoy the landscape of the street, the beautiful buildings, or the statues, to enjoy the art of his city, the greenery, the parks, the people. Instead of all that, he has to take care of his safety in order to protect himself from the dangers all around. Man, the creator of the city, has lost his freedom in it, he is safer out in the countryside than downtown, and this has happened for the first time in history.

If we look at this problem from the point of view of society, we must recognize that our society, no matter how many technological means it has at its disposal, no longer operates with the same efficiency as in the past, especially in the small scales. We can now travel very easily from one continent to another, but if we want to go to the airport we lose a great deal of precious time, and we commute daily for much longer periods than we did before. We thus deprive ourselves of precious time previously at our disposal for our leisure, for our relaxation, for our thinking, and probably for our creative thinking.

Looking at this problem from the point of view of shells, of our buildings, we can recognize that they are better inside than in the past, but if we look at them from the outside, we must recognize that we have not developed the beautiful architecture of the past. We cannot even look at them, as we are in grave danger if we try to approach a building unaware of the dangers in the street.

Our networks are sometimes much better than in the past, our telecommunications are much superior to anything ever created in the past and so are many of the other networks, such as electricity networks, but in spite of that, they do not lead to a better city. We have only to think that in spite of all these networks we must travel longer hours. We cannot cross a highway at the point we want, and although we drive on the highway at higher speeds than before, it takes us longer to visit a neighbor living on the other side of the highway. We have not developed networks that satisfy all human needs.

The result is that our city turns into a city that is not as good as the city of the past. The growing city creates many problems in its central area; the downtown area receives pressures from a much greater organism and it can no longer function properly. Many trucks serve the commercial area and have to wait long hours on all sorts of streets. They have to. park in the squares, the area turns into a lower-class habitat. As a result of this, the higher income groups once living in the central city have abandoned it and have been followed by people of lower income groups. These again have been followed by others of even lower income groups, and the final result is that the weakest income groups of the city move into the central area. As it happens, the greatest majority of the lowest income groups in the United States belong to a special racial group, the Negroes. The downtown area has turned into a Negro area and therefore, the problem that started as a structural problem turned into a problem of the succession of economic and social classes, and finally, has turned into a racial problem.

As long as we leave our cities to suffer structurally, to be inappropriate cities, the problems will be added to each other and the structural, economic, and racial will be intermixed into a very difficult and confusing situation from which all citizens will suffer and certainly and especially those of the lowest income groups who, by necessity, fall into the worst areas of the city—we can call them "pits." As long as we allow our cities to be full of pits, who else will fall into them but the weakest groups?

WHY WORRY ABOUT THE CITIES OF THE FUTURE?

If the cities of the present are as bad as we have described them, why should we start worrying about the cities of the future? Should we not concentrate our attention on the cities of the present? These questions require a very clear answer. It is too late to do anything for the cities of the present. Tomorrow morning is the future; this is even more true for the weeks, months, years, and decades to come. Our life will not be spent in the cities of the present, but in a combination of the existing cities of the present and the cities of the future, which we shape with every decision we take at every moment. If we bring one more car into our city, we create more difficult traffic problems. If we extend the city into a low-density suburb, we need a much greater number of more expensive facilities and we all have to pay for them. No matter who pays for the construction of the facilities, we all have to support the organizations, public or private, that supply us with water, electricity, telephones, and other amenities. We have also to pay more for cleaning of these new parts of the city, for their maintenance, for policemen to guarantee our security. For every aspect of the life of the city we create, we share responsibilities and we share benefits or disadvantages.

The city of tomorrow will be almost like the city of today, with some few additions of people and cars and perhaps a few dwellings completed and a new shop opened. The city in a week from now will be different from the city of today. This is true for the city in a few months, years, and decades. Depending on how long we intend to live, we have to decide to think more and more about the future. If we end our life tonight, we may be allowed not to think of the city of the future only if we do not have children, descendants, friends who will survive our death. I do not believe that any reasonable person can be allowed any longer not to think of the city of the future.

We then have to ask ourselves whether worrying about the city of the future will help us in any way. To this our answer must be very positive: the city of the future depends on our own decision and action. Unless we worry about it, we cannot help it. If the city of the future is built by us, if we decide to build a better city, it will be built. If we decide to build a worse one, again it will be built; or if we leave things to go on as at present, we may have a very bad city indeed. These are really the prospects. Not only is the city of the present very bad, but what we build today is leading to a city which will be much worse than the present one. No matter how we extrapolate our present trends, no matter what kind of calculations we make, we are led to the conclusion that the city of the future that we are building will be much worse than the city of the present.

If this happens, then man himself will not be the same any more. I think we must understand that we shape our cities and then they shape our way of life, as Winston Churchill very aptly pointed out. But what we must add is that we are shaping them at random, and consequently, forming a way of life at random. In this way there is no hope of creating a better city.

To create a better city we must take the situation into our hands and be able to measure the city in terms of human values. To show this I will take as an example the way in which we spend our time, as that is our greatest commodity. Man, in this case the average American citizen, spends 76 per cent of his lifetime at home (males 69 per cent and females 83 per cent) and only 24 per cent away from it. He spends 36 per cent sleeping, 20 per cent working, and 10 per cent eating, dressing, and bathing. He is left with 34 per cent or one-third of his life for leisure, pleasure, thought, and so forth. It is this one-third that constitutes the basic difference between man and animal. But males between 20 and 59 have only 20 per cent of their time free, of which one and one-half hours for some or three hours for others are spent in commuting. This means that they are deprived of one-third or two-thirds of the free time that makes the great difference between man and animal, a free citizen and a slave. This waste of our great commodity results from the fact that nobody conceives our way of living and nobody facilitates it. Anyone is free to waste our energy by forcing us to wait for longer periods at red lights, or to cover longer distances by releasing his contaminated exhaust in our street. I think that it is important for us to remember that our houses and our factories, and the corresponding way of living or producing, follow our decisions, but not so our cities. No businessman would allow me to sell him a factory plan without guaranteeing special economic performance, and he would not allow any machine to be included if it did not serve his goals. This is not so in our cities, and then we wonder why they are so bad, or perhaps we get used to them and consider the great, unreasonable heap of produce we are building around ourselves to be the city of man of which we can be proud. It is time for us to understand that the way we are going to live in the cities of the future ten, twenty, fifty, one hundred years from now—we, ourselves, our children, and our grandchildren—depends on the decisions we take now. We cannot only predict; we have to decide. We cannot only complain; we have to build.

ALTERNATIVES FOR THE FUTURE

If we are aware that we should worry about the city of the future, and that this city depends on our decisions, then we must start thinking about what alternatives we have. The alternatives are as many as there are people who make decisions, as there are combinations of decisions that people can make. Each person decides about his house; many decide about the facilities, the transportation systems, the factories, the public buildings; and some decide about plans of parts of the city, others about other parts, some about the airports. The final result is that, depending on the thousands and millions of decisions taken every day about our cities, we may come up with different cities in the future. To understand how different the cities may be, we can try to understand the two basic alternatives we have.

To understand where we are going, I had to have the abilities of a prophet who could look into the future and foresee. I do not have these abilities. I can only present the two alternatives as given to me when I decided to ask this question in the most ancient oracle of the world, the oracle at Delphi. After all, I had to make some use of our ancient civilization and the facilities that it presents. I went to the oracle, and I explained my worries about the cities of the future, the chances for the survival of our civilization, the chances for man to survive with all his values, or to lose them, even my worries about the forthcoming death of the great cities and the civilization itself which we have created within them. I then waited for an answer outside the temple of Apollo. The answer I received was quite typical of the oracle. Scratched on a red tile I could read "Prospects of survival no death of city." Knowing how the oracle enjoys playing with people's agony, I tried to place the missing period, and came up with two different oracles. The first read, "Prospects of survival no. Death of city," and the second, "Prospects of survival. No death of city."

Confused, I sat on the marble steps until finally I decided that I would combine modern technology with ancient imaginative capacity and explore the various alternative prospects opened to me by both oracles. Thinking about this problem I came to some conclusions which I can present in three points: The first oracle; the second oracle; and my conclusions.

If I follow the first oracle, then in order to get from Athens to San Juan, Puerto Rico, I have to travel to New York first and then to San

Juan. I take the helicopter from Delphi—why not? Since their noise does not allow me to be quiet even in Delphi any more, I might as well make use of them to get to the rocket-port of Athens; from there after a 20-minute flight we land at the rocket-port of New York City. From there I board an airplane, which, after a 30-minute wait in line for the take-off and an even longer one for landing, takes me to the newest airport fifty miles from downtown; from there I take a taxi. Guided by radar and great projectors through the thick smog, we reach my hotel after four more hours. In this way I discover one of the new laws of transportation: the shorter the distance, the longer the time needed to cover it. We are allowed into the hotel after proving that we do not belong to any gang.

Visiting the city is not easy. Some friends recommend the use of a mask, others a guide, and all insist that we should not stay out after sunset. Nobody is allowed to walk any more since the machines make it both a luxury and very dangerous; walking is better, someone tells me, in the special "walking hall" of our hotel where a moving carpet gives the opportunity to those who want to move without using their weakened legs to do so, and where special mixtures of oxygen are provided for better breathing. It is specially recommended for those coming from nonconditioned areas.

I am informed that to go out would mean less anyway, since buildings have no windows, shops exist only inside buildings, flowers and trees survive only in the mountains, and people do not like to meet foreigners. The children are suffering from all sorts of phobias, while adults have no time for new contacts, since work, commuting, and visits to their doctors and psychiatrists exhaust them completely.

I then have to follow the same course again from my hotel to the airport, to the rocket-port. It takes me several hours to reach the rocket-port, one minute to fly to the rocket-port of Puerto Rico far outside San Juan, and then we pass through the same difficulties in order to reach the helicopter. After waiting in queue we enter a helicopter that takes us to the roof of the very large hotel near the beach where we now are. We have to wait for several minutes to land on the roof. We are taken to the elevator, we show our identity cards and we are allowed to descend three floors to the entrance lobby. After checking in, we are taken downstairs to the rooms, as people have now decided to enter their buildings from the top. There is no chance of driving in the streets, as there are so many people who come to San Juan in order to breathe some fresh, not bottled, air that it is forbidden. There is only one chance: to fly by helicopter. However, as soon as we enter our rooms we see on the wall television that there is no prospect for a breeze today, the air is so contaminated that we had better stay inside our rooms; however, the good prospects are announced that fresh northerly winds may allow people to walk out to the beach. In one of the next two days people are warned that they should not consider swimming in the ocean because of the great waves of oil floating all around the island. You can look at the ocean, especially at night when the discoloration is not so apparent, but you should always avoid entering it. It now becomes clear that the first oracle is true: there are no prospects for survival; our city is dead.

It is time to try my second oracle and again follow the same course from Delphi to Athens, to New York, to San Juan. From the temple of Apollo I *walk* back to my hotel, enjoying the peaceful surroundings, the yellow flowers, and the birds, including an occasional eagle, which flies above and below me into the valley. I explain that I have to take the shortest road to New York and am told that the plastic bubble will be ready for my journey in ten minutes in my room.

I hang my clothes in its special closet, I close its door, I lie on its armchair, fasten my belt and push the buttons "Destination: New York, Waldorf-Astoria Hotel," "Meal at 1300 hours. G. T.," "Passport Greek 12.31.62," "Do not disturb please," and "I am not interested in the steward's stories." The fact that my bubble is taken to the basement of the hotel and through an underground tube to the rocket-port, loaded on a rocket, unloaded in New York, and by another tube, guided to my hotel room, is known to me, but not felt.

The only thing that matters is that after seven hours of work and rest, a knock on my door informs me that I am in my room at the hotel. I walk out of my bubble. I refresh myself and go out for a walk on Park Avenue, which, deprived of the cars, now all underground, in its main and center part exhibits the greatest collection of sculpture ranging from Rodin to Henry Moore under the trees, among the flowers. This exhibition is flanked by marble-covered pavements for those who walk along the avenue and by covered sidewalks for those window shopping.

I am in the midst of the best that mankind has created, and I feel happy that industrial progress has allowed me to enjoy New York City as much as the wilderness of the Greek mountains. In both, we find that nature and society have developed their best expression. Buildings and networks of transportation systems and other facilities have developed to the point that they only serve man without imposing their existence on him.

After spending several hours enjoying downtown and New York, I enter my room again, I order my plastic bubble, I turn the buttons labeled, "Destination: San Juan, Intercontinental Hotel, no meals, no messages." In one hour's time the sign on my door shows that I have reached my hotel room in San Juan, I open the door, I find myself in a big room with a very big verandah, full of sunshine, overlooking the blue ocean. I put on my bathing suit, I walk down to the beach and I throw myself into the fresh water of the ocean. The second oracle is true: there are great prospects for survival; there is no necessity for the death of our city.

I can now make my third point. If such are the alternatives before us, if the future of our cities leads either to the death of the city and civilization, or to their survival and renaissance, and the creation of a new civilization, we must be ready to take action in our hands. This action should not be parochial, however; it should not be short-sighted. This time our action has to be guided towards one goal: to create a better city for man. To achieve this we must proceed in a systematic way. We should be limited neither by time nor by space. It is too late to think only of the next few years. We cannot turn the tide in a few years. The problem has been created over a few generations;

we will need enough time to overcome it. Also, we should not limit our space to our neighborhood or to our suburb, or to our downtown area only; they are all parts of one system. We must look far out in time and in space.

WE MUST CONCEIVE THE CITY OF THE FUTURE

We cannot be limited, we said, in space or in time. We must try to understand where we are going and where we should go. This requires the conception of the total city of the future towards which we are tending. In order to be realistic, we must understand that we have failed in the past because we still think in terms of our small villages or our small cities or even our metropolis; but we are already moving from the metropolis to the megalopolis. In Japan, for example, one big city is taking shape from Tokyo to Osaka, with a length of 600 miles; another such city is taking shape from Boston to Washington, including New York, Philadelphia, Baltimore, and many minor cities with a total length of 600 miles; and several other such cities, more than ten, are beginning to take shape on the other continents. It would be completely unrealistic to believe that these are the last big cities to be created. On the contrary, we can predict now that many more such cities will be created and at the end they will all be interconnected into one huge universal city which we call "the ecumenic city" or *ecumenopolis.*

This is the only realistic prediction, because it is completely utopian to believe that the population of the earth will stop growing today, or that birth control efforts will have results tomorrow morning. Realistic studies show that even if birth control decisions were taken today by the United Nations, it would take one generation's time to implement them throughout the world. If so, the present population of the earth, which is almost 3.5 billion people, would be 7 billion by then, and because of the ongoing forces, the population of the earth would level off at 12 billion people—even if, we repeat, we could pass a birth control decision today for the whole world. As this is not

176

Ecumenopolis in 2100 A.D.

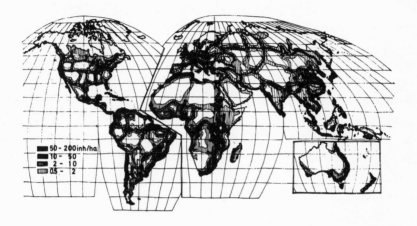

probable, it is much more realistic to think that the population of the earth will continue growing beyond the 12 billion mark and will reach a level of 20 to 30 billion or, according to some projections, 40 to 50 billion people. We limit ourselves to a reasonable assumption of 30 billion people, almost ten times the present population.

Such a conclusion has led several people to say that we will have ten times the urban problems that we have today, but this is completely wrong. These people forget that really big urban problems are presented for the almost 1.5 billion people living in cities (two billion more live in the countryside), and as the rural population would not increase, the total urban population in the future will be of the order of 28 billion people or almost thirty times the present one. This means that the average city of the world will be thirty times larger, that its area may be sixty to a hundred times larger, and that it may have many times more problems, as the problems do not increase in proportion to the population or to the area, but much more than either the population or the area does.

Because of such an expansion, our urban areas will be all interconnected into one system, leaving long uninhabited corridors mostly in the great plains, near water resources, and in the most beautiful parts of the world.

We will be, therefore, faced with a universal city huge in proportions in relation to the present one, with many more people, much greater numbers of machines, but with far greater economic forces and technological and scientific knowledge. This is the city of the future with which we will have to deal. This is the city that may be the ultimate phase of urban development on our earth, or at least the next phase at which humanity will stop for many generations, many centuries, or many thousands of years to come. It may live as long as the small cities of the past have lived—for almost 6,000 to 7,000 years—by which time humanity may enter a new phase of its evolution and develop something which is completely inconceivable today.

For all practical purposes, we can think of this universal city, or ecumenopolis, as the next step towards which we are heading, a step at which humanity will remain for a very long period. Our real problem is to make this a human city in which man can survive, and not allow it to destroy man and lead him to his end as a biological, or at least as a civilized, individual.

This city will be extrahuman in dimensions. No man, no individual using his natural physical abilities, will be able to cross it, will even see it. It will go beyond the horizon even if we fly high up in the air, as it will surround the earth. If we allow all present forces to develop on the basis of existing trends, then this city, which will be extrahuman, will also turn inhuman and man will be unable to survive. Our great challenge is, instead of letting the extrahuman city become inhuman, to turn it into a human one. Can we achieve this? We certainly can.

We are now in a position to know what the human scale is. We know how far man walks or cares to walk. This has always been in all civilizations, even in the present one, a distance of over one kilometer, or two-thirds of a mile, which can be covered in ten minutes' time. We are in a position to know from how far man can see a monument. The most distant one he has created in a beautiful city is the Arc de Triomphe in Paris which can be seen from a distance of no more than two kilometers. We know from what distance man is interested in seeing his buildings, how large his squares should be to correspond to the human scale and to let him enjoy them. In this way we are in a position to create a human unit within an extrahuman surrounding. The human unit is a circle with two kilometers diameter or, expressed in an urban way, a square with a side of 2000 meters. This is the area that corresponds to all the famous cities of the past, to Athens of the Periclean age, to Florence at the time of Michelangelo, to Paris and London within their old walls. This is the unit within which people care to walk today, the unit within which they can easily reach the shopping area, the unit within which they can have facilities corresponding to their daily life, a unit corresponding to 30,000, 50,000 or 60,000 people.

We are, therefore, now faced with two facts: that the universal city will be extrahuman in dimensions, and that the human dimensions lead to a small unit which we could call the "human community," or the cell of the extrahuman city. Thus, we reach a very important conclusion: that the extrahuman city should consist of human communities that should serve as its cells.

If we now think how nature has developed big living organisms, we will remember that this is the way in which such organisms have to be created, by the repetition of cells which form much greater, much more complex organisms. This happens to our body and to many other organisms in nature. This is a natural solution. We now have a conception of the city to come and a goal for how to shape it to serve man.

FROM THE CITIES OF THE PAST AND THE PRESENT TO THE CITY OF THE FUTURE

The conception of the city of the future does not guarantee an understanding of it in all its parts, much less the understanding of how we are going to move from the cities of the present to the city of the future. But this is our task. To achieve it, we must understand that today we inhabit all sorts of cities, from very large to very small, and all sorts of parts of cities, from very ideal ones (at least in accordance with some criteria) to very ugly, depressed ones which are in great trouble. We must, therefore, develop the ability to understand two things:

1. What is the role of our city or the part of the city we live in?
2. What are the problems of our city or the part of the city we live in?

Like good doctors we need to make a proper diagnosis of our case in order to advise how far we can go towards remodeling the part of the city we live in, or reshaping it completely so as to make it more satisfactory for our needs.

Like good doctors, we must learn that there are many kinds of diseases and that every disease has a different importance for every patient. There are no general therapies that we can implement. Every case needs its own therapy after a proper diagnosis. What we can now see is that we have several categories of cities, several categories of diseases, and that we must understand them and act correspondingly.

I will take a few cases. Let us first start with the small cities. No matter whether many people live in the big cities and whether many more will live in them, there are more than two billion people who live in small settlements. Maybe people will be prepared to ask me what is the value of the small cities, why in the light of the birth and growth of the universal city are we interested in the small cities. Why do we so frequently defend them? Is it because they are small and need defense, or is it a matter of social policy? These explanations do not make any sense at all. I think that arguments in favor of small cities are justified because they have a value for their own inhabitants, a value for those of the big cities, and a value for our entire population and civilization.

Their value for their own inhabitants is quite apparent: if they provide shelter, employment, and community life of a quality not available in the big cities because of their deficiencies, then small cities do have a great value for their inhabitants.

Their value for the population of big cities is due not only to the services they provide for them—for example, as centers of primary production—but also to the fact that they do preserve human values, which are gradually being lost within big cities. This is a very important factor that is almost always overlooked: at a moment of a great crisis, owing to the development of the ecumenopolis, for which we are not prepared, it is in small cities that certain values can be preserved. Let us not forget that our big cities are in such a crisis that we do not know whether they will be saved—although I myself believe that they can be saved. In case humanity fails in big cities, our survival is entirely based on the small ones.

Finally, their value for the entire population and civilization is due to the fact that we all depend on a very complicated system consisting of an enormous number of human settlements, ranging from the largest to the smallest ones. We cannot allow any part of it to disintegrate without endangering our possibilities for survival. How do we know that big cities can survive without small ones? It has never happened before, and we are not allowed to let it happen now without being aware of the repercussions to our welfare.

Because of the value of the small cities, we have to protect them so that they will not be absorbed by the expanding cities or isolated and abandoned somewhere in a stagnating area. In these two cases we must act differently. If our small city is very close to a big, expanding one, we cannot avoid the development of the forces which will lead the big city to surround the small one. What we can avoid, is to allow the big city to choke the small city to death by its pressures. We must use the great opportunities that the big, expanding city gives the small city, but we must protect it from losing its own values. This can be worked out on the basis of a new plan by which many important centers can be created all around the small city in such a balanced way that the small city will not have to grow beyond the limits of its interests.

If its roads, for example, and its shopping center can serve 100,000 people, there is no reason why it would be allowed to grow to

200,000 people, so that we can see its center declining and then have to spend millions and billions in urban renewal, which in many ways is a wasted effort. If, on the other hand, the small city lies far beyond the limits of the services of the big cities; if, because of this, it is stagnating, we must find ways to revive it and let it grow to the point allowed by its inner structure, allowed by its inner interests. This has to be financed by the overall community, as it is in the interest of humanity as a whole to allow the small cities to survive, no matter where they are.

If we now move to the big city we can examine two parts of it: a typical suburb and finally its central downtown area. In a typical suburb we may witness phenomena of great shifts of forces. A small suburb may have been created as a garden city, a residential community, a dormitory town. If so, and if it satisfies its own needs, it is in very great danger of having its nature changed by many expanding forces. These may be an expanding downtown area, or expanding systems of transportation networks or expanding industries. We must, therefore, reach the conclusion that a suburb has to protect itself, has to have its own plans in order to have all the advantages of a big metropolitan area without suffering from its dynamic growth. In particular, this requires the definition of the role of the suburb and the determination of how much this role is properly served by the existing structure.

Finally, we have to look into the downtown areas of the big, expanding cities and of even the small expanding cities, if they grow with a great dynamism. In such areas we can see a great decline of all values, of buildings, of investments, of human values. If this has happened, it means that the center cannot withstand the new pressures and that it is breaking under the pressures of an expanding urban organism. If so, then we have to take measures to protect the downtown area from additional pressures. This means not allowing more people to visit it, using all sorts of different transportation means, because then the center will be choked to death.

I think at this moment we should remember that many organizations that try to bring more people into the downtown areas, without caring how they bring them in and how they satisfy them, may well achieve results opposite from those expected. Bringing more people in requires greater highways and more parking spaces, which may dislocate shops indispensable for the proper operation of a big downtown shopping area. Shopping streets may lose half of their buildings to parking lots; this creates a discontinuity in the shopping area and unsatisfactory window-shopping. As a result of this, people and functions move out of the downtown area.

The solution in such cases does not lie in decentralization, as is usually recommended. This is completely wrong. By decentralizing several functions, we split them all apart. We suppose that the central area serves as the headquarters of the financial, commercial, and cultural life, but there we fail. We cannot decentralize. In order to save our downtown areas in most cases we have to "new-centralize." By this I mean the creation of new centers of an equal or even of a higher order than the existing one. If we have a city with one million people who come to the downtown area for their central services, and if its streets and other facilities cannot handle any more people, why should we bring more? If we allow only minor shopping centers to be created all around the area in the suburbs, great pressures will still be exercised on the downtown area. If another million people are added in the periphery, then the downtown area will suffer from pressures of two million people. If instead, however, we create one new center for one million people, and when the population grows to three million people, a new center for this additional third million, for the fourth one, and then also, someday, a center to serve all centers of one million people, then we can be satisfied that the old center will not suffer from additional pressures. It will serve its people, it will not lose its values, it will not see shifts in population, changes of economic and social classes and segregation between them and between the different racial groups. In such a case, we do not lose in any investment, be it economic, technological, cultural, or aesthetic. The new-centralization will solve our problem.

183

By these three examples we have seen that, depending on the type of city and on which part we are interested in and its problems, we must follow different courses in order to make it a part of the whole universal city of man; a part which will best serve the citizens of the small unit as well as the whole system to which it belongs.

WE MUST BUILD THE CITY OF THE FUTURE

Conceiving the future of our cities—the bad road they have taken, the good road that they may take—conceiving the future of every single city or part of a city of ours, is not enough. We must build the city of the future.

In order to build the city of the future we must be realistic, we must develop a process, and to achieve this, we must follow a certain order that has been taught us by practice. I present here the main points that we should always keep in mind, should always remember as imperative steps for a proper process leading us from the desire to have a better city of the future to the moment when we will actually live in it.

First, we have to start the process. It is not enough to speak about the problems of our cities, to speak about the need for planning, to speak about the need to start this process, and even to complain about the others who do not start the process—the city authority, or the state or federal government or the international agencies that do not take care of our settlements. We have to start somewhere. It is much better to start at the proper level with the responsible authorities, but if we are unable to do this, we must start anywhere, with a private group. We should not forget that Greece's reconstruction after the war was prepared by a private group working underground during the occupation under grave danger, and therefore the country was prepared to rebuild its economy and reconstitute its normal life. We should not forget that many valuable efforts are those of private citizens who have conceived proper solutions, have started the battle. We should not forget that the press can play a very great role and that private groups in many cities, downtown businessmen, associations of businessmen, citizens' groups, religious groups, and others have been able to start the process, to move gradually from the overall conception to the plans and execution.

Second, we must organize the plan on a proper basis. Any plan will not do; many plans are quite disastrous. I still believe that most of the cities of the world implement plans that are quite negative in relation to the future of the life of the citizens. They only guarantee some alignments, some rights of way, but not the future life of the city, which is the important goal.

To organize our plans, it is important to see every urban organism as a whole. We cannot study three-quarters or half an organism as we very often do because of the administrative boundaries. It is time we had the courage to understand that our cities build systems of cities and that we have to take one whole system and study it very carefully. If we cannot study the whole area—for example, if we are a small citizens' group in one part of a big metropolitan area, certainly we cannot face all the problems of the millions of citizens—then we have to select the largest feasible unit, but make sure that it has reasonable and rational boundaries and reasonable connections with the units above it. This means that we should select a community of a certain order, let us say a small neighborhood, but up to its natural boundaries and we must make sure that although we study only our community, we understand the total of the forces exercised on it by its surroundings.

This means that we have to start a process of organized planning and we can start it from both ends, either from the whole to the parts which is preferable, or if we are only concerned with parts or only able to face the parts, then start with the parts and try to understand the whole system to which they belong. It is unreasonable to design, plan, be prepared for a small community that we may conceive as an ideal residential community, and because we have not taken care to isolate it from the systems of highways, to protect it from expanding industry and commerce, to see it choked under these influences.

The same is valid for the time dimension. Many people tend to prepare a plan just for a short period of time, for a one-year, three-year, five-year, or ten-year period. But our buildings, our action will survive even our own generation and will go beyond it. Why should we try to understand only what will happen in the next three years or five? It is imperative that we try to conceive the future of our city, our settlement, our community for as long a period as possible, plan for it on broad lines, and then plan in detail and construct what we can afford today. Planning for the future and building for the present is what we need.

Third, we must present the plans properly. We must show clearly the problems of the present and the problems of the future in terms that can be understood by the people who will use the city and the settlement. It is needless to present facts if we cannot interpret them and show them as problems related to everyone's life, if we cannot express the design in economic, social, political, technological, or cultural and aesthetic terms.

To show our plans properly we should not show the solution. We should show the alternatives that exist, and not the solutions we prefer as a group or as planners. We should present the solution that the citizens prefer in accordance with our understanding of their needs. If we express our plans properly then the people will be able to say: well, these were not our intentions, we do not care to have straight streets or curved streets, we care to go to our home in a much shorter time, or we care about the safety in our streets. This is the operational expression of a plan. We have then to make recommendations for each of the alternatives on the basis of the goals set by the community. We must classify the alternatives. We should not give our subjective opinions, but our objective opinions. We should only give, and we should finally show that the best alternative, the best solution for the citizens is only a certain one, if our assumptions about the citizens' wishes are right. In this way we allow everyone concerned about the plans for the future to follow our reasoning, from the collection of the facts to the evaluation of the problems, the conception of the alternatives, their evaluation, their comparison, and the selection of the best solution.

Fourth, we must see that the plan is approved; otherwise it will have no value at all. It will be just an intellectual exercise of some interest to some scholars someday—if it is good, because it may also be a bad plan. But even if it is good, this will never be recognized, this will not have any value, unless it is implemented. The plan must be approved by the citizens of every city or community or region, depending on the area we have studied. We should not try to convince them that our plan is a good one, we must let them be faced with the facts and the reasoning resulting from them. Practice has proved everywhere that it is better for the citizens to have a plan they believe in than a plan set forth by a planner. A plan that is not implemented has no value at all; a plan which is approved by one autocrat without the understanding and support of his people will be abandoned as soon as this autocrat ceases to exist.

Fifth, we must implement the plan. We must have the courage to create the future instead of waiting to see it happen. Our cities should not just happen, they should be created by those who are able to conceive them and to build them. To implement the plan we do not need to implement it today; what we need today is a decision to implement it, but it will take years, decades, maybe centuries to implement the whole plan. Let us not forget that even isolated works of art, such as an ancient temple or a medieval cathedral, have not been built at once. Sometimes it has taken generations to complete them, but the community believed in them and finally built them. We must have an even greater patience and the ability of the right time perspective when we speak about cities. We cannot build the cities of the future today, but we can lay their foundations.

Finally, we must see that the plans are developed and evolved in accordance with the needs of life. Actually, when we have a plan, we should insist that it be understood in order to be respected. We should insist that it is implemented as properly conceived, and not changed by everybody in accordance with his wishes. But this statement alone could be misleading. This could be valid for a small unit of our settlements, especially a monument, whose purpose and whose relationship to the life all around it does not change, but this is not so for a city. A city must have a plan that will be respected; but, as the life of the city changes beyond expectations in many points, we should develop the ability to respect the plan that we have implemented and at the same time to change it when necessary. The key for this is the understanding of the plan. This is why it is so important that the plans be understood by people. If so, they will respect and implement them until the plans cease to serve the goals for which they were set, and then the community, by the same process that led to the creation of the plan, will effect its transformation. If we understand this point then we can rest assured that the plan will not remain a hindrance to the life of the community but will constitute the guide, shaped in a certain form and reshaped when necessary, causing the minimum of inconvenience and leading to the maximum of satisfaction.

8

Clarence Walton

Concluding Note: Re-creating the City of Man

The word "city" once suggested "civility" and those character-istics of culture and politeness which attend that term. In a generic sense, the "City" referred to the financial and commercial district of greater London. In ways partially symbolic and partially real, the nexus between the cultural and commercial cores of the city remained in a healthy condition. Today, however, "city" means crisis—a crisis oc-casioned by past neglect, present indecisiveness, and bewilderment over future explosions of undetermined magnitudes in size, density, violence, and the like.

The deepening sense of worry is magnified by a certain nostalgia for a "one-time" city as a place with clean boundaries, impressive town-gates, graceful cathedral spires, stately town hall. London, Paris, Bruges, and Berne carry the clear stamp of generations of craftsmen who built the churches, town halls, and marketplaces to serve, func-tionally and aesthetically, the religious, political, and business needs of man. These visible signs were the city's center and the city's heart.

Today the urban core is a depressing slum—more a cancer than a healthy organism. The very word itself is as distasteful as any word in the dictionary: slum "links both slop and scum and also has the cadence of slush, slovenly, slut, slump, slug, slubber, slob, slub, sludge, slummock, sledge, and slutter. Slum gives its meaning the moment it is uttered."[1]

Unlike their European counterparts, American cities lack the age-old qualities that came from artistry, slow adjustment to slow changes, and the affections and fierce pride of those who, born in the one city, are destined to live and die there. In contrast, the American nation includes thirty-five million people who are on the move annually; as a consequence the city allegedly becomes the temporary home for passing people. This psychology of mobility suggests that, for many, the American city is a quasi-tourist attraction where transients take what they can and leave when they must.

Clearly the picture is overdrawn. Every city, including the American city, is, in Charles Abrams' felicitous phrase, "the palimpsest on which man's story is written, the record of those who built a skyscraper or a picture window, fought a pitched battle for a place, created a book-shop or a bake-shop that mattered. It is a composite of trials and defeats, of settlement houses, churches and school houses, of aspirations, images, and memories. A city of values as well as slums, excitement as well as conflict; it has a personality that has not yet been obliterated by highways and gas stations; it has a spirit as well as a set of arteries and a voice that speaks the hope as well as the disappointments of its people."[2]

THE CITY: EUROPEAN AND AMERICAN PATTERNS

It is this keen awareness of common characteristics in both European and American cities, as well as cognizance of their singular differences, that has led Peter Hall to make his comparative study between the continent and North America. To Hall, European urbanism, starting with the premise of an urban culture, held that "cities have achieved a special position in fostering and housing that civilization; that cities, as ancient repositories of culture, should be protected from decay; that our vanity, in the strict sense, is a virtue which should be preserved by the planners."[3]

The American vision started with the same European concept of an urban culture but in the transatlantic crossing (and, more likely, during the twentieth-century urban explosion), it has moved towards a new form expressed in the suburban culture. If there are relatively few defenders of the philosophy of suburban living these defenders are articulate and sturdily committed to the so-called "western American school" of the 1960's. The premise of this group is that a particular set of urban functions and of urban relationships need not be accommodated within a particular urban shape. America is a mobile people and, therefore, the notion of easy access and rapid movement to important contacts is all that really matters. Decentralized functions on the freeway allow Los Angeles, so the argument goes, to function as effectively, perhaps even more effectively, over vast areas than the traditional centralized metropolis. Whether Los Angeles represents the collapse of a great 5,000-year urban tradition or the birth of an entirely new posturban culture is open to debate; but it is clear that the "urban place" is being challenged by the "nonplace urban realm."

Defenders of the suburban culture reject arguments of commentators like Riesman and Whyte who see the suburb as a center of stifling conformity, civic indifference, and sophomoric taste; Hall points to studies by Jaffee, Berger, Gans, Wattel, and others which prove that suburbanites are not conspicuous consumers, not slaves to fads, not organization men, and not conformists who are ripe for any take-over. If Professor Hall carefully analyzes the difference between continent and the newer American cities, he finds a similarity in a very unexpected place—Las Vegas. Las Vegas is the only city in the world whose skyline consists neither of buildings nor trees—only signs. But the signs, in Tom Wolfe's words, are themselves "adorned with a symmetry and excitement of their own." And in this architecture of signs Hall discovers quality similar to Versailles, another one of the few architecturally uniform cities of the West created specifically for the pleasures of the affluent.

This willingness to concede great importance to the variety, mobility, and flexibility of contemporary American life is a recognition of the vitality of the North American continent and the originality of its creators. But in what might be interpreted as a subtle warning, Hall reminds Americans that the European metropolis may have lessons to teach Americans. Chief among the lessons are the need for greater degrees of positive intervention by government agencies in the whole process of metropolitan growth. We are asked by Professor Hall to reconsider an important question: whether natural and spontaneous growth, determined primarily by physical location and economic need, can serve effectively for the future, or whether the future city is to be deliberately shaped along preconceived designs by urban planners?

MODEL-BUILDING AMERICAN STYLE

Margaret Mead's essay reflects the anthropologist's almost instinctive preference for spontaneous and natural growth. Her model of the small city becomes a reference point as well as a convenient benchmark against which to measure other models, such as a *microcity* like St. Cloud, Minnesotá, a *metropolitan* city like New York, and a new city like Columbia or Reston. Many would agree with Professor Mead that the small city (150,000-250,000) offers the best in human living. Agreement may come because of the appeal exerted on the American minds by the rural romantic or because historians have often adorned the small city of the 1900's with a richness and charm that, in fact, they may not have possessed. Agreement may also be stimulated by awareness that a "dinosaurus" effect sets in not only for biological organisms but for human and industrial organizations as well when any entity reaches a certain size. Whatever the reasons, there is a clear conviction that all people simply cannot tolerate living in centers of tremendous population densities and that diversity of urban types is needed because of the diversities among people themselves.

Professor Mead is too much a realist to conclude that the small city is necessarily the epitome of all that is good in human living. She draws a contrast between a mythical Center City, which approximates the ideal, and a Border City, which almost totally negates the ideal. Unlike Border City, an impoverished mill town hampered by absentee management in business, Center City is a model of local initiative, cosmopolitan interest, and civic pride, which, however, sometimes masks a certain complacency.

A hallmark of the successful small city is the role played by voluntary associations, such as the various service clubs (Lions, Kiwanis, and Rotary), the City Improvement Society, the Society for Support of the Arts, and similar organizations. There are in the small city many outlets for the individual to satisfy his instincts for interpersonal group relationships free from constraints found in governing bodies. Perhaps the gravest threat to the successful small city is a complacency that could remove it from the mainstream of American life. It has no large-scale slum, no deteriorating schools, no inadequately supported health facilities, and no housing shortages. This catalogue of the successful small city's "lacks" spells out rather precisely what large metropolitan areas have in superabundance.

In addition, Professor Mead suggests the wisdom of building a city's strength on a specialized economic activity. There are, of course, historical prototypes for special-interest cities: Pittsburgh, with its steel industries, Scranton with mining enterprises, Grand Rapids with furniture. Because these are vestiges of an industrial era found in a time when the country is moving towards a postindustrial society, Professor Mead suggests that there is a persuasive logic in believing that the small city of the future may have as its special interest, for example, research-and-development activities. The growth of the electronics complex in the Cambridge area, which draws strength from Harvard and from M.I.T., is one illustration of this development. What the Mayo Brothers achieved with their world-renowned clinic is another example.

There is also clear evidence that a leisure-oriented society of the future will create communities catering to different kinds of outdoor sports. For example, completion within the decade of the Tocks Island Dam in the Delaware River will give to the Philadelphia and New York metropolitan areas the largest man-made reservoir east of the Mississippi. This sportsmen's delight will attract millions, and the small cities within this area (Stroudsburg and Port Jervis) may have futures far brighter than anything that marked their past. Port Jervis, today a moribund ex-railroad center, can capitalize on its new resource to achieve a high degree of prosperity; whether it has the entrepreneurial skill to develop allied attractions such as summer theaters, art centers, ballet, and the like remains to be seen.

That leisure-time pursuits will become a big business for some communities is a prophecy supported by a small change in our social habits—the coffee break. Development of this social habit in the nation has had enormous significance in the State of New Jersey, which handled over $2 billion worth of coffee shipments in 1967 and which has attracted the world's largest coffee makers, such as Maxwell House, Chock-Full-O'-Nuts, Bosco, A & P Coffee Service Division, George Washington Coffee, Hills Brothers, Nestlé's, Chase and Sanborn, and others. One usually thinks of New Jersey as a special-interest state for chemicals and pharmaceuticals, rarely as a coffee distribution center. If an eight-minute interval for leisure has had such widespread impact on one area, one can speculate on what an eight-week interval for vacationing will have on others.

The Mead proposition, therefore, is extraordinarily attractive. It simply recognizes what economists call the "law of comparative advantages," which holds that the most productive arrangements are those in which organizations and individuals specialize within activities for which they are best equipped. But weaknesses need also to be identified. Specialization tends to alter the organism that specializes.

For example, a city that specializes in manufacturing is a city that gives large sections of its resources to plants, industrial sites, and housing, and relatively little to shopping centers or to institutions such as colleges and hospitals. Once this pattern has been established it becomes difficult to maintain the kind of balance that the small city requires. There is a further danger. In a world of accelerating change comparative advantages are continuously being eroded. The capacity for local leadership to change with changing demands may be as effective as Corning (cited by Dr. Mead as a model) or as ineffective as Lowell, Massachusetts.[4] In short, if one great danger to the large city is a complexity of activities that make meaningful interrelationships difficult, the danger of the small special-interest city is a narrow economic base that makes rapid adjustment to new changes unlikely.

OTHER MODELS: THE MICROCITY AND THE NEW CITY

Lest we become too preoccupied with models represented by the small city and the metrocity respectively, it is useful to remember that intermediate sizes also exist. Minnesota, for example, which is about median of the total population among states of the union, has the fourth largest number of governmental units, the largest number of townships, and the third largest number of school districts. It is claimed that the state has numerous microcities which are "unorganized for political action in the legislature and devoid of anything but the most sketchy picture of their collective condition."[5] Leaders of these microcities feel often that present concerns with metropolitan problems may result in severe inequities to them. For example, Mayor Edward Henry of St. Cloud, Minnesota, a fairly typical microcity, has argued vehemently that taxpayers of his community provide the major part of the county's tax base but receive little or no attention in the county budget. The state legislature has passed tax programs that take little or no account of the special needs of the microcommunity. He found that the Minnesota Legislature recently passed a law dealing with state-wide dairy and bakery operations which required that every municipality accept state standards, but the standards are established not by the Department of Health but by the State Agricultural Department which is concerned with farmer's markets rather than city-dweller's health.

The foregoing illustrates problems that the microcity is beginning to feel when state legislatures start to focus on problems related to the metropolitan crisis. It suggests quite clearly the need for a balanced approach because, if the large city has been victimized in the past by rural domination of state legislatures, there is now fear in the small communities that an unhappy history is about to be repeated in reverse.

Thus far we have been primarily concerned with existing cities. The explosive population growth means that already crowded areas will become even more crowded and that some innovative steps must be taken to accommodate the explosion. There emerge opportunities for the development of "new" cities such as Reston, Virginia, and Columbia, Maryland. The latter provides an especially interesting case study.

James Rouse's tale of the creation of Columbia is a story of great entrepreneurship. Initial projections called for the purchase of 14,000 acres of land at a cost of some $20 to $24 million; but what made the effort distinctive was the manner in which plans were evolved. The Rouse company summoned into group meetings fourteen knowledgeable people representing psychiatry, sociology, education, religion, and the like. From group discussions (the group, incidentally, was not asked to develop a report, but rather to talk in depth about man and his needs) emerged the plans on which the company moved. In Columbia is an interreligious group working to form a corporation that will buy property to house services by various sects; housing will be at a level to accommodate the relatively low-income family as well as families from middle- and upper-income brackets. By design Columbia seeks to become a truly cosmopolitan city by incorporating within its environment a membership from various economic and social strata.

Efforts to assure survival for the microcity and success for the preplanned "new" city deserve critical and sympathetic attention. Their successes will do much to assure a richly diversified form of human living by the year 2000. Failures could mean that reconstituted city cores, hopefully strong and healthy in the future, would be surrounded by decaying peripheries.

METROPOLITAN CENTERS AND THEIR PROBLEMS

There is no question that the really intense problems in the United States reside in the metropolitan areas. Today some 135,000,000 Americans live in the urban areas—twice the number of a single generation ago. Fifteen years from now the figure is expected to double again when 80 per cent of the nation's people will live in cities that occupy only 10 per cent of the country's land areas. It is precisely this overwhelming role, coupled with historic neglect, that makes metropolitan areas prime targets for consideration.

In some respects New York and Chicago are no different in their problems than Caracas and Buenos Aires, or London and Paris, or Calcutta and Tokyo. All great urban centers are concerned with extraordinarily rising demands for health services, for housing, for jobs, for physical safety in homes and on the streets, and for a measure of serenity undisturbed by what might be called noise pollution. Because problems for American cities are compounded by racial considerations, analysis of urban needs in the United States cannot be carried out without special recognition of these racial elements. A comment on each of these problems (health, houses and jobs) clearly reveals their close relationship to the problem of race in American life.

Health Needs   There are about 180,000 practicing physicians in the United States today—practically the same number that were available in 1929. Whereas in 1939 only 30 million Americans (representing 25 per cent of the population) had income to pay for the full health-care services then available, today over 155 million Americans carry voluntary insurance against hospital costs, and practically all of these people are insured to some extent against surgeons' and doctors' bills. It is no exaggeration to say that the market for full health-care services is about five times what it was forty years ago.

Does this mean a fantastic shortage of physicians? Most people think so, but there are some mitigating factors. Abolition of house calls has practically doubled the number of patients a single doctor can handle; more important than the changes in practice is the fact that there are now close to three million other people in auxiliary services of the health field. Fifty per cent of these work in hospitals, one-third are employed in the pharmaceutical and medical supply industries, and one-sixth are retail pharmacists or visiting nurses.

But these mitigating circumstances cannot blind us to the fact that the poor are still inadequately cared for. In the American urban scene the poor are heavily Negro. Infant mortality among nonwhite babies is almost three times as high as that of white babies; life expectancy is significantly lower for American nonwhites: there are few doctors in poverty areas of a city.

There is, happily, an obverse side to the coin. There is no question that the paramedical professions will represent one of the vital growth elements in the service industries of the future and that the big cities will be acutely concerned with the quality and standard of education for paramedical career. "Paramedics" will be the key people on a team working under the leadership of a trained physician. And the care will occur most frequently in the hospital. Forty years ago the community hospital was a charity institution for the dying poor; forty years ago almost all American babies were born at home; and forty years ago almost all the bronchial pneumonia patients were cared for at home. Today, 98 per cent of the babies are born in hospitals and a bronchial pneumonia patient is always hospitalized.

Careers in paramedical professions will be open to nonwhites on an unprecedented scale as health centers in urban communities become key institutions of the society. Around the health center can be

198

clustered other activities and institutions that can transform the slum into a satisfactory complex.

Incidentally, it should be noted that despite remarkable advances in hospital care, these advances invariably are designed to make repairs after damage has been done. In the future there will be enormously greater concern for preventive measures. Yet few people are thinking of the organizations necessary to carry out preventive services; nor are probing questions being asked on how such activities should be financed. With medicine becoming not only a healing art but a "health-giving art," the nature of hospital service within the large urban community particularly will have to be thoroughly re-examined.

The effect of noise on health serves as another illustration for the need of preventive services. What noise pollution does in the urban environment is hard to determine. Some experts have claimed there is a causal relationship between exposure to excessive noise over a period of time, and the incidence of allergies, heart disease, gastro-intestinal disorders, and migraine headaches.[6] Others have argued that the evidence is far from satisfactory in demonstrating any causal relationship between prolonged noise and physiological disturbances.[7]

While the debate rages, there is little doubt that noise levels are intensifying. In New York City today they exceed the levels permissible for many factories,[8] and this seems to be true despite the fact that New York City has long had comprehensive antinoise ordinances which prohibit the creation of "any unreasonably loud, disturbing and unnecessary noise—of such a character, intensity, and duration as to be detrimental to the life and health of any individual." But as is so often the case it is difficult to police the law and enforce it effectively.

Perhaps the simplest, yet most accurate, statement regarding urban noise control was made by the editors of the Columbia *Journal of Law and Social Problems:*[9]

> The problem of the increasing menace of urban noise must be faced now. The ineffectiveness of present solutions in handling the threat . . . demands a re-evaluation of our present legal structure. . . . The most im-

portant task is to make the public aware that offensive noise can be controlled and angry *enough to do something about it*. Without the active support of the public, all the planning and programming, all the conferences and statements by public officials are little more than "so much noise."

Housing   Closely related to the problems of urban health are the issues of housing and jobs. These are considered by many to be the primary causes of frustration among the city residents, and particularly among the urban minorities. The "opinion spectrum"—running from the Kerner report, to an AFL-CIO labor declaration in the *American Federationist* (October 1967), to statements by General James M. Gavin, Board Chairman of Arthur D. Little Company)—all testify to the need for an imaginative response by government and by business to the growing needs for housing and for jobs, especially among the urban minorities.[10]

If we examine the pattern of migrations, it is clear that the countryside still sends millions of people to the city every decade. But it is also clear that the majority of migrants to American cities are coming from other suburban areas. The great mass movement of Negroes from villages to southern cities is coming to an end after a fifty-year cycle. It has been estimated that in an average year, five million of over twenty million nonwhite Americans have moved from one building to another; of this group four million have stayed in the same county. The long-distance migrants, therefore, are a small minority among all nonwhite movers. The number of Negroes, for example, moving directly from the rural South to the Northern and Western big city is shrinking, and the Negro migrant now typically moves from one Northern or Western metropolitan area to another. The result of these migrations is the concentration of nonwhite populations in the central sector of every major metropolitan area. During the 1950-60 decade the percentage of nonwhites in Washington jumped from 35 to 55 per cent; in New York from 10 to 15 per cent, and in Cleveland from 16 to 29 per cent. In 1980 it is estimated that in Washington the percentages of nonwhites will reach 95 per cent, Cleveland 55 per cent, Chicago 44 per cent and New York 25 per cent.

How are these people housed? Normally the "turnover" is the basic process by which low-income groups improve their facilities. Between 1950 and 1960 almost a million metropolitan housing units went from white to nonwhite occupancy whereas fewer than 100,000 went from nonwhite to white occupancy during that same period. Therefore, it would seem that as new construction proceeds there are grounds for optimism that the needs of the minorities will be increasingly met. But the optimism rests on no sure base.

We know that between 1950 and 1960 substandard housing was cut from 2.8 million to 2.3 million and that the percentage of substandard housing for Negroes declined from 73 per cent in 1950 to 44 per cent. The comparable figures for white families are 32 per cent in 1950 and a drop to 13 per cent in 1960. Clearly the low-income groups, and the minorities particularly, did not share substantially in the improved housing conditions during the 1960's, because the real gains accrued mainly to middle- and upper-income groups.[11] Slum dwellers continue to suffer most acutely.

One study showed that in the hard-core slums of Newark, most slum-owners were found to have little interest in property improvement. If housing demand increased, the owners felt that they could hold the line and reap a profit; if housing demand decreased, the owners became fearful of making any substantial investment.[12]

The government's response has been the Model Cities program in which Congress was asked to provide $537 million—an amount that San Francisco alone needs to renew the substandard housing within its city limits. The corporations and the entire business community may make important contributions in this area. General Gavin has suggested the need for a government-industry "special purpose corporation" to be formed along the lines of the Communications Satellite Corporation. This new corporation, created with government help but independent of it, would seek to bring the organizational skills of private industry into management of funds. In Gavin's view, an Urban Experimental Corporation (URBX) could bring job stability to the construction industry because there would be a guaranteed number of housing units to be built each year. A guarantee, in turn, would provide incentives to both industry and unions to modify present restrictive practices on material use and to employ building technology which, according to some estimates, could reduce the cost of a $16,000 home to $8,000 within a five-year period. Gavin declared that housing units now renting for $134 a month could be rented for $67 a month. And he cited a California experience where a systems approach to school construction reduced the cost of school ceilings from $3.24 per square foot to $1.81 within a six-month period.

Just as Gavin advocates a COMSAT type of enterprise, it is certainly feasible for the private sector to consider other significant social innovations through the creation of a corporation built along URBX's line but funded and managed *solely* by private industry. This private corporation could take a comparable area for housing improvements in another section of the country, and at the end of a given period an audit could be carried out to discover which form of organization leads to better results. Because there has been so little social innovation along such lines, the business community has an enormous opportunity to contribute to the solution of a major urban problem.

Employment   Jobs are a third absolutely crucial factor in urban society. Labor leaders have already demanded the immediate creation of a million jobs in the public sector area to employ the hard-core unemployed. There are another million jobs necessary in the private sector, and the Kerner Commission said that these jobs must be created within the next three years. The same Commission urged tax credits for on-the-job training that involved extra costs for private employers, and it called on private employers to eliminate all racial discrimination in job opportunities and in job promotions.

The significance of jobs can, therefore, hardly be overstated. In one study this question was asked: "Why did you move?" The consistent answers were the offer of a specific job or a desire for a job. Net migrations to an area corresponds very closely to the region's income level and to its production of new jobs. An analysis of net

202

migration from 1870 to 1950 shows that during this period Negroes as a group, even if they had less to hope for, responded more sharply to changes in economic opportunities than did whites.[13]

Many employers operate on the myth that the new migrant, and especially the new Negro migrant, is less educated and less equipped for jobs required by a technological society. Yet Professor Tilly of Toronto has pointed out that an important result of comparisons he made between those who were in an urban ghetto for some period of time and those more recently arrived, lead to an ironic conclusion for those business leaders and city Fathers who wish to speed the departure of Negro migrants from their towns. Said Tilly:[14]

Such a strategy would be a very good way to depress the average level of qualification of the city's Negro population. It would probably increase the proportion, if not the absolute number, of the Negro population heavily dependent on public services.

If business would seek to welcome these recent Negro migrants then a significant start could be made toward easing the transition. Where the job opportunities will lie becomes a significant question. Certainly the service industries will become increasingly important. In New York City there will be an expected decline during the present decade of nearly 140,000 manufacturing jobs. At the same time medical and health care comprise one of the city's major industries so that a very substantial need exists for employees trained in the paramedical services. Health services rank as the third largest employer in the country (with only agriculture and construction employing more workers), and the health service industry remains labor intensive, with approximately 70 per cent of the hospital's budget going into manpower.

Safety   A fourth factor in the urban scene, violence, has been an intrinsic part of the American past. At the turn of the century a German journalist touring this country, Ernest Otto Hopp, remarked on the ubiquity of the American gang: "At any hour of day and through many hours of the night, in snow and in rain, the gang may be seen there at the saloon, inspecting the passer-by, spitting and smoking, not quite drunk but not quite sober." If gang violence is not new to the United States, it is clear that the problem has a new urgency. In his 1968 State of the Union Message President Johnson declared that "there was no more urgent business before this Congress than to pass the Safe Streets Act." The very size of the large city, the opportunities for anonymity, the pressures created by population density, and a host of related factors, combine to make crime and its detection inordinately difficult. Gang violence, therefore, is only one part of the picture.

In a recent analysis of serious crimes in New York it was found that the police were able to solve only 80 per cent of the homicides, 50 per cent of the rapes, and 48 per cent of felonious assaults. A third of all violent crimes were committed in only six of the city's eighty precincts; according to the *New York Times,* Harlem, southern Bronx, and Bedford-Stuyvesant are the high-crime areas. These acts of violence are often crimes by individuals and are not necessarily related to those organized crimes which in 1966 allegedly "grossed more money than General Motors, Ford, Standard Oil, General Electric and United States Steel put together."[15]

Again, convenient myths identify the minority as major culprits for rising violence. One popular explanation for urban rioting places the blame on a "black phenomenon" when, as a matter of fact, from 1917 to 1960 there were no major Negro riots; the record reveals that all severe riots were begun by the whites and were aimed at the Negroes—as the Chicago and Detroit riots of the 1940's amply demonstrated.

There seems to be the further assumption that the minority migrant is especially footloose, solitary, and irresponsible. Yet in a study of 900 Negro boys from a high-delinquency section of Philadelphia, Leonard Savitz discovered that youngsters brought up in the city had delinquency rates 50 per cent higher than migrants from elsewhere.[16] Although most studies demonstrate that crime, delinquency, family instability, divorce, and illegitimacy are concentrated in areas of high mobility, they fail to show that the mobile persons in these areas actually create the disorders. A more logical conclusion is that a depressing environment, inadequate or overcrowded housing, and high unemployment are the major contributing factors to the crime rates in the ghetto areas.[17]

Perhaps there are two harsh facts that need realistic understanding by the American people: (1) If the Kerner Commission Report is correct, then America is a racist society with all this implies in terms of housing and job opportunities and diminished opportunity for social and cultural achievement; and (2) the fairly standard American belief that Negro life today is not much different from that of the early migrants, and that therefore the Negro will move into the mainstream of American society in a few generations, is not true. The "melting pot" theory fails to account for the fact that discrimination seems to have worsened in recent times and that Negroes feel a greater degree of alienation from American life than before.[18] A great deal more must be learned about the process of assimilation. Quite clearly, if assimilation means anything, it means the closing of the gap between the outsiders and the rest of society, yet the improvement in absolute terms for jobs and for housing opportunities cannot obscure the fact that, in relative terms, the gap between the whites and nonwhites has widened.

It is for these reasons particularly that the urban crisis in American life must be viewed in the dimension of race. It is for these reasons that the message of Professor Tilly needs to be underscored when he says: "Migrants as a group do not normally disturb public order; their arrival does not lower the quality of the city's population; they place no extraordinary demands on public services; and they do not arrive exceptionally burdened with personal problems. *These things happen to them later.* The difficulties faced by inhabitants of ghettos and by cities containing them are not to any large degree products merely of migration."[19] The real challenge is to open opportunities for the migrant in terms of better jobs, better housing, better schooling, better health care, and the like.

If the problem, then, is not migration as such, migration does underscore other problems related to assimilation in terms of the opportunities the city may offer or deny the minorities. And this is almost exclusively an urban problem.

CITIES OF THE UNDERDEVELOPED SOCIETIES

Preoccupation with the urban crisis as the priority matter on our domestic agenda may blind us to the fact that the urban crisis is even more acute in the underdeveloped areas of the world; four-fifths of the world's future population increase will occur in areas least able to sustain them. And yet, just as we were able to draw interesting comparisons between different styles developed by American cities, so also may we draw important distinctions between city development in the Asian world and city development in Latin America.

Perhaps, as Dr. Matsushita suggests, the city of the future is Tokyo, because Japan sits as a highly indusrtialized oasis amidst a desert of poverty. Nothing illustrates the dimension of desperation more poignantly than Calcutta, the subcontinent's largest city and major port. This city, which accounts for 30 per cent of Indian bank clearances, 42 per cent of India's exports, and 15 per cent of Indian manufacturing, is slowly strangling to death because its nearly eight million people are ill-housed and ill-fed. So enormous is the problem that a team of American and British planners declared that the collapse of Calcutta would "be a disaster for mankind of a more sinister sort than any disaster of flood or famine."

As a consequence, there will be an enormous push from peoples in underdeveloped communities of Asia to migrate to a more developed community like Japan. Anticipated for Tokyo is the formation of a new kind of city-state that recalls the historic models of Athens or Sparta, Venice or Genoa. But there is an enormous difference. The new Asiatic city-state of Tokyo would be international in scope; it would draw from all nations of the world, fusing cultures in new variations that make the "melting pot" experiences and the problems of assimilation in America relevant to new areas. These are some of the themes expressed in the essay by Dr. Matsushita.

Because of the magnitude of the problem, it may well develop that Tokkaido as an international center will require international help if serious disequilibria are to be avoided on the entire Asian continent. This may well mean that the United Nations will see city-building and city-renewal as crucial as its peace-building functions. Indeed the two may become inseparable.

If the Matsushita essay is properly concerned with the Asian problems, the probings of Victor Urquidi into Latin American cities provides a basis for useful comparisons. Urban planning in Latin America is predicated on the needs of the middle class, but even this premise is becoming ineffective because land values have risen so astronomically that the middle and lower classes are simply denied access to the housing market. As a result, shantytowns are sprouting quickly all over the peripheries of all the large Latin American cities, and their people are ill-housed, ill-policed, and ill-serviced.

If Americans are so concerned with urban problems that they are even now seeking remedies in law, so too must the law of Latin American societies take into account what might be called the squatter problem. Heretofore, property rights have arisen in Latin America in much the same way as they have generally come in North America—through purchase or bequests. But there may be need for legal reforms to grant to squatters some legal control and interest in property.

At this point one is impelled to draw an interesting parallel between the recommendation offered by Professor Urquidi and that offered recently by Arthur Holden, a New York architect, who urged changes in American law to permit Negroes living in slum areas to develop property rights.[20] Holden pointed out that existing legal usage governing real estate values makes any improvement to property an improvement attached to the real property and, therefore, a gain in value for the property owner. There is no consideration of what is due to the creator of the new property values. Under the new formulations squatters would be given an opportunity to develop their rights to property, and Negro tenants who make improvements would have a vested interest in that same property.

Urquidi argues that an end must be put to present Latin American urban patterns that reveal small splashes of wealth interspersed among "shockingly grim slums and ugly surroundings." Latin America is beset with the problems of the *premature* city, which may well be a preview of a future *noncity* unless current developments are changed. When it is recognized that slum dwellers and the "marginal community" dwellers (the squatters and the criminals) can number from one-quarter to one-half or more of the populations of the larger cities in India, Turkey, Peru, Venezuela, Iraq, Senegal, and many other countries, then the staggering proportions of the problem of the noncity begin to emerge.

It is equally clear that there can be no substantial and enduring improvement in urban living if there is not a concomitant improvement in the rural areas. Currently, land-tenure systems are inadequate and grievously unjust so that people move to urban centers, not because new techniques have made them a human "surplus," as in the advanced countries, but simply because the land cannot feed them. Yet cities, which are traditionally the centers of industry, have experienced a drop in manufacturing from 35 to 27 per cent between 1948 and 1968. Furthermore, employment in tertiary activities is relatively higher in Latin America than it was in Europe or the United States during a similar stage of industrialization. What does this all mean? It means that the flow of migrants into Latin American cities is resulting in rapidly growing urban underemployment; one estimate indicated that as many as 8.2 million people were in a condition of "disguised unemployment" in Latin America in 1960. Within the next two years this unproductive and subsistence-income sector of urban centers is expected to reach close to eleven million people. Latin America may have as much need for international support in urban planning and financial cooperation as Asian cities.

What the multinational corporation might do in Latin America is hard to predict. That it can have a crucial role is clear when Professor Urquidi remarks that "the housing problem seems to raise serious doubts about urban life, in general, but the latter is, in turn, largely a reflection of inadequate economic development coupled with unduly high population growth. The answer to urban development and the future of the presently underdeveloped city, must be sought, consequently, in the broader context of economic growth and social change, rather than in the city itself or in its own structures."[21] Unless far-ranging and constructive steps are taken in concert with the developed nations of the world, the grim prophecy of an urban doomsday is likely to be fulfilled.

THE CORPORATION-CITY NEXUS: A SECOND LOOK

The introductory essay began with a citation from Plato's *Republic,* and it is singularly appropriate, therefore, that this analysis should find its conclusion in the observations of a contemporary philosopher from Greece: Constantinos Doxiadis. United to Plato by the instinct for a good society, Doxiadis takes as the measure of the future human community the measure of man himself. Instead of asking "What is man?," Doxiadis asks "How does man spend his time?" And the concept of the life of "thirds" is revealed: man spends roughly one-third of his time sleeping, another third working and eating, and the remaining third in leisure. It is the final third that constitutes the basic difference between man and animal.

The question, therefore, for the city of the future appears to be this: How shall we fashion and cope with the universal city, an ecumenopolis that will serve the basic needs of man and allow leisure time to be used for genuine human creativity? The ecumenopolis will be inhuman and impersonal unless we take into account the deeply human and personal needs of the individual. One must literally create a personality for this "extrahuman" entity, which no man, through the use of his natural physical abilities, will be able to cross or to see as a whole.

Despite the mammoth proportions of the universal city, we know enough about the nature of the "human scale" to plan carefully. We know from what distance a man can see a monument; we know that he walks about two-thirds of a mile in a ten-minute interval; we know that the human unit is a circle with a two-kilometer diameter. And from these observations Doxiadis believes we can create a living unit within which people can walk comfortably, can easily reach the shopping area, and can have facilities that provide the necessities of daily life. This unit would be a center for 30,000 to 60,000 people, which would comprise part of a "system of cities."[22] Only centers at least partially self-contained and sufficiently diverse to provide for the basic needs of individuals comprising it, should be built within the system. From them will come the aggregation which is the ecumenopolis.

Perhaps here is struck another important role for business, because Doxiadis is talking of systems analysis as an organizational device for providing diversity in unity. Historically, the American corporation was premised on the notion that unity emerged from a uniformity. The emergence of interstate corporations like General Motors, Standard Oil Company of New Jersey, and Du Pont in the nineteenth century led their hard-headed executives to decide on adaptations in organinational structures. Typical is General Motors, which moved quickly between 1920 and 1925 to create organizational patterns that carried implications far beyond the automotive industry itself. As Professor Alfred E. Chandler, Jr., has noted, these automotive executives were proud of what they had achieved. In describing their new organizational methods and techniques they formulated new principles and philosophies of management.[23] The genius of business was thus not simply expressed through technological innovations but in organizational innovations as well.

In city-building great organizational skills are required as much as great sums of investment money. Governments have the major role, but the business community must also respond. Indeed James Rouse noted that city-building was one of the world's most important businesses and that there was no industry comparable to a General Motors or a United States Steel in this area. Rouse has noted that his own experiment with the new city of Columbia proved that profit-making and social-building could go hand in hand. Meanwhile, other executives are asking whether or not real profits can accrue to corporations that undertake work in metropolitan rebuilding. Henry E. Arnsdorf, Vice-President of Prudential Insurance Company of America, has defined business philosophy of the future in terms of "a moral commitment as a responsible corporate citizen to help repair the damage." He recognizes that this philosophy is not fully shared by others whose management philosophy is largely restricted to the profit motivation, but in his estimation, "the future success of the enterprises will depend on a *conversion* to the new role of business for which I have been speaking."[24]

Business, and especially the mature corporation, does represent a pool of resources that can be put to work on urban development as one of the major problems of our time. It is also apparent that if it is important to seek to aid the teeming millions of the underdeveloped nations, that aid will have to deal concretely and directly with the urban problems of Latin America, Asia, and Africa. If private initiative and if private-public cooperative efforts are both useful and desirable on the national scene it would seem to follow that the same combinations can also be applied on the international scene. For it is clear from the essays incorporated within this volume that the city of the future in the underdeveloped society will have no future—will become a non-city—unless there is mounted massive and sustained help from the more developed nations of the world.

NOTES

1. Charles Abrams, *The City as a Frontier* (New York: Harper & Row, 1965), p. 19.

2. *Ibid.,* pp. 16, 17.

3. Hall, *supra,* p. 99.

4. Eli Ginzberg, ed., *Manpower Strategy for the Metropolis* (New York: Columbia University Press, 1968), pp. 30-37.

5. Edward L. Henry, "St. Johns Establshes Small-City Study Center," *Minnesota Municipalities,* III (February 1968), p. 2.

6. "Hearings on Noise: Its Effect on Man and Machine," *The Special Investigating Sub-Committee of the House Committee on Science and Astronautics* (86th Congress, 2D, Second Session, 1960).

7. Donald L. Broadbent, "Effects of Noise on Behavior," in Cyril M. Harris, ed., *Handbook of Noise Control* (New York: McGraw-Hill, 1957).

8. See report of Dr. Samuel Rosen to the Conference on Noise Control in New York City as carried in the *New York Times,* March 19, 1967.

9. March, 1968, p. 119.

10. James M. Gavin and Arthur Hadley, "The Crisis of the Cities: The Battle We Can Win," *Saturday Review,* February 24, 1968, pp. 30-34.

11. Bernard J. Frieden, "Housing and National Urban Goals" in James Q. Wilson, ed., *The Metropolitan Enigma* (Washington: U.S. Chamber of Commerce, 1967), pp. 148-193.

12. George Sternlieb, *The Tenement Landlord* (New Brunswick, New Jersey: Rutgers University Urban Center, 1966).

13. Charles Tilly, "Race and Migration to the American City," in Wilson, ed., *The Metropolitan Enigma,* p. 130.

14. Tilly, *loc. cit.,* p. 131.

15. *Crime in the Community—A WNBC-TV Report* (New York City, 1968), p. 4.

16. Leonard Savitz, *Delinquency and Migration* (Philadelphia: The Commission on Human Relations, 1960), p. 16.

17. See also the study of the Pennsylvania Prison Records, which demonstrated that the imprisonment rate was much higher among Negro natives than for the Negro migrant, whereas for whites it was the other way around. See J. L. Kingman and E. S. Lee, "Migration and Crime," *International Migration Digest,* III (1963), pp. 7-14.

18. The "melting pot" theory is effectively argued by Oscar Handlin, *The Newcomers* (Cambridge: Harvard University Press, 1959).

19. Tilly, *loc. cit.,* p. 141.

20. Arthur E. Holden, "Self-Help in Minority Housing," *Focus* of Columbia's School of General Studies, I (Spring, 1968), pp. 16-18.

21. Urquidi, *supra,* p. 86.

22. For strictures on our usual association of economic growth with the growth of big cities, see J. G. Williamson and J. A. Swanson, "The Growth of the Cities in the American Northeast 1820-1870," in *Explorations in Entrepreneurial History,* IV (1966), pp. 3-69.

23. Alfred D. Chandler, Jr., *Strategy and Structure: Chapetrs in the History of Industrial Enterprise* (Cambridge: The M.I.T. Press, 1962), p. 160.

24. "Poverty and the Business Community," *The Journal of Business,* XVI (May 1968), p. 2. A similar view was expressed by E. Sherman Adams (Senior Vice-President of the First National City Bank) "Banks and the Urban Crisis," *Banking* (June 1968).

Biographical Sketches of Contributors and Editors

Margaret Mead

MARGARET MEAD is Curator of Ethnology at The American Museum of Natural History and Adjunct Professor of Anthropology at Columbia University. She has also lectured widely in colleges and universities in this country and abroad. She has spent many years among various South Sea peoples studying their cultures, but she is also interested in studying contemporary cultures in the light of perspective gained from studies of small, homogeneous, stable societies, such as those she has worked among in the South Seas. Dr. Mead has written widely, both for a professional audience and a more general one. Her many books include *Coming of Age in Samoa, Male and Female, New Lives for Old, An Anthropologist at Work, People and Places, And Keep Your Powder Dry,* and *Continuities in Cultural Evolution.* Recently she has turned her attention to the problems facing the city of the future and has written a number of penetrating articles in this field.

Masatoshi Matsushita

MASATOSHI MATSUSHITA is an authority on international law. He was formerly President of Rikkyo University, where he had taught since 1929. He has served on the Japan Defense Council for the International Military Tribunal of the Far East and also as Chairman of the National Council for Peace and Against Nuclear Weapons. Dr. Matsushita is also on the Commission of the Churches on International Affairs, established by the World Council of Churches and the International Missionary Council. He is Chairman of the Japan National Congress for Education. He was elected a member of the House of Councilors in the Japanese Diet in July 1968, to serve for six years.

Victor L. Urquidi

VICTOR L. URQUIDI is President of El Colegio de Mexico, where he helped to establish a research program on economic development and population change. For many years he was a research economist in the Bank of Mexico and an adviser in the Mexican Ministry of Finance. He has worked with the United Nations Economic Commission for Latin America. His current interests lie mainly in the relation of higher education, science and technology to economic development and in the impact of population growth. Mr. Urquidi is the author of several books, among them *Free Trade and Economic Integration in Latin America* and *The Challenge of Development in Latin America,* and is the founder of a new journal *Demografia y Economia,* published by El Colegio de Mexico.

Peter Hall

PETER HALL is Professor of Geography and Head of the Geography Department at the University of Reading, in Great Britain. He is a member of the advisory council that assists the British Government on the regional planning of Southeast England. He has actively engaged in a number of regional planning projects, including the direction of a team on the plan for a new town in mid-Wales, published by the British government in July 1966. He is currently a consultant to Britain for a joint Anglo-American research project for comparing patterns of urban growth in the megalopolis region of North America's eastern seaboard and its British equivalent. Professor Hall is the author of several books, including *The Industries of London, London 2000,* and *The World Cities.*

James W. Rouse

JAMES W. ROUSE is President of the Rouse Company, a mortgage banking and real estate development firm with executive offices in Baltimore, Maryland. His company has financed over a billion dollars in real estate development through its various offices and owns and operates more than $200 million in real estate projects in eight states and Canada. The Rouse Company is the developer of the new City of Columbia between Baltimore and Washington. Mr. Rouse was formerly a member of President Eisenhower's Advisory Committee on Housing and Chairman of the Subcommittee that recommended the urban renewal program embraced in the Housing Act of 1954. He participated in the formation of ACTION (American Council To Improve Our Neighborhoods). In 1955 he was engaged by the District of Columbia to lay out a workable program of urban renewal for the City of Washington. He has lectured on various aspects of housing, design, and community development at Johns Hopkins, Harvard, and the University of California.

Constantinos A. Doxiadis

CONSTANTINOS A. DOXIADIS is one of the world's most noted urban planners. He is President of Doxiadis Associates, Consultants on Development and Ekistics, in Athens. His company has participated in planning and development that now affects the lives of some sixty million people over the globe: in Iraq, Lebanon, Libya, Pakistan, Rio de Janeiro, Ghana, Baghdad, France and Zambia, as well as the United States and Greece. Dr. Doxiadis is particularly known for his theories on Ekistics, the science of human settlements that concerns the interrelationship of man with his environment. He serves as a consultant to the United Nations, the International Bank for Reconstruction and Development, the Agency for International Development, the Inter-American Development Bank, various governments and other international bodies. His books include *Ekistic Analysis, Architecture in Transition, Urban Renewal and the Future of the American City, Between Dystopia and Utopia,* and *Ekistics, an Introduction to the Science of Human Settlements.*

Richard Eells

RICHARD EELLS is Director and Editor of the Program for Studies of the Modern Corporation, Graduate School of Business, Columbia University, and is also Adjunct Professor of Business. He is President of the Arkville Press and is a trustee to several foundations and a consultant to various business corporations. Professor Eells has published widely on the emerging role of the modern corporation in our society. His books include *The Business System* (edited with Clarence Walton), a three-volume study of the conceptual foundations of modern business, *Corporation Giving in a Free Society*, *The Meaning of Modern Business*, *The Government of Corporations*, *Conceptual Foundations of Business* (with Clarence Walton), *The Corporation and the Arts*, and *Education and the Business Dollar* (with Kenneth G. Patrick).

Clarence Walton

CLARENCE WALTON, the Dean of the Faculty of General Studies at Columbia University since 1964, also holds an appointment as Professor of Business at Columbia. In 1966 he chaired both the University's Executive Committee and the Advisory Council that were created to recommend ways to make effective use of a $10 million Ford Foundation grant designed to assist Columbia University's efforts to meet urban-minority problems. Dean Walton is the author of numerous books and articles. His recent works include *Corporations on Trial* and *Corporate Social Responsibilities*. With Richard Eells he edited *The Business System,* a three-volume study of the ideological foundations of modern business. Earlier he and Professor Eells coauthored the McKinsey award-winning book, *Conceptual Foundations of Business.*

Index

Index

233